EYEWITNESS IN VIETNAM

A BACKGROUND SPECIAL

Eyewitness in Vietnam

Hugo Portisch

Translated from the German by
MICHAEL GLENNY

DUFOUR EDITIONS
CHESTER SPRINGS
PENNSYLVANIA

959.704
P

Illustrations

[All photographs by the author]

I

FOR the last twenty years the name of one country has appeared almost daily in the world's headlines: Vietnam. For the last twenty years every ricefield, every square mile of jungle of this country has been fought for. Thousands, indeed tens of thousands of Vietnamese and French, Foreign Legionaries, Americans, Australians, New Zealanders, Koreans, Filipinos and many more have lost their lives in this country.

This war in Vietnam has been called the 'dirty war'. Dirty not only because it takes place in the mud of the ricefields and the jungle; dirty not only because it is primarily an unorthodox war—a war of treachery and horror; but dirty because the world believes—and often rightly so—that this war only serves the interests of the great powers and that the wretched Vietnamese population is being made to suffer for it.

It is also a war which has seemed likely to bring the world more than once to the brink of a major atomic war. The danger that one shot too many in Vietnam might make the generals in the USA or in China press the red button seems very real. That is why we are all involved. This war concerns every one of us.

I have been in Vietnam. I have seen the war there. Not only the war in the front lines, which are not front lines at all; not only the terrible man-to-man duels in the thick of the Vietnam jungle; not only the shattering American air-strikes, not only the rockets and the napalm bombs: I have also seen the other war—the fight for the hearts and the minds of the Vietnamese peasants.

Until recently it was rightly said that this was a war which only the communist guerrillas, the Vietcong, were fighting and which only they could win. And they could only win the war with weapons. But this is no longer the case today. 'This war,' explain American diplomats in Saigon, 'will not be decided by weapons alone. A military victory will only be conditional. The real struggle is on a social, economic and political level. If we cannot win it on that level, then we will have lost.'

This is undoubtedly true. But the West, and the USA, have reached this conclusion rather late. Now that it has been realised, however, a social, economic and political offensive has been launched in Vietnam, alongside the American war effort, which puts even the Marshall Plan in the shade. The total expenditure is much less because Vietnam is a small country compared to Europe, but its significance lies in its policy implications and in the manpower effort involved in carrying it out.

Whilst an armada of thousands of aeroplanes and helicopters, an arsenal of millions of rockets, bombs and shells and armies of well-trained troops have been deployed to turn the tide in the military struggle against the Vietcong, only one step behind them hundreds of civilians are moving into the liberated areas to do battle for the hearts and minds of the Vietnamese population.

In South Vietnam people no longer simply talk about 'the war'. Nowadays the talk is of revolution. The war against the Vietcong is only marginally a military confrontation. It has been somewhat tardily declared to be a national revolution and an attempt has been made to give this revolution form and meaning.

I have also seen some of the efforts to put this revolution into effect. No one can tell as yet whether they will be successful, but one thing is certain: the USA, whose diplomacy ten years ago was still conceived in uncompromising terms of black or white, friend or foe, this USA which marched resolutely over the 38th parallel to punish the North Koreans, this USA is now showing a surprisingly cautious diplomatic hand in Vietnam. Not a single word is said against the communist regime; there is no threat of an invasion into North Vietnam. The supply routes and the training camps of the Vietcong on this side of the 17th parallel are bombed, but so far the bombing attacks on North Vietnam have still been restrained by Korean-War standards.

An effort is thus being made to save the opponent's face as long as possible, for this is the opponent with whom they will one day have to sit down at the conference table. They have learned that if their opponent's prestige is not protected to a certain extent there will be no hope of negotiating with him later. That is one of the reasons for the restraint shown towards North Vietnam.

The second is aimed at keeping China and the Soviet Union out of the shooting, in other words to prevent the Vietnamese conflict from triggering off a third world war—even to the extent of overlooking certain Vietcong supply routes. North Vietnam should not feel forced to protect these routes with her own troops, thereby limiting the North Vietnamese military commitment and making her less likely to call for Chinese 'volunteers'.

Behind the American soldiers in Vietnam there are not only the civilian experts on rural development, schooling, health, agriculture and road construction, not only the revolutionary reformers whose aim is to conquer 'the hearts and minds' of the people. The American troops in Vietnam are also accompanied by political advisers, who are diplomats (or 'political commissars', as they are half-jokingly called by correspondents). No commanding officer of a US army battalion can start a military operation in Vietnam today without the permission of these political advisers. No pilot takes off today from one of the American aircraft carriers in the Gulf of Tonkin in a raid on North Vietnam without having first received from a civilian political expert precise orders on what he may bomb and what he may not. The war in Vietnam has thus become a unique operation.

It must be emphasised that no one can tell whether these methods are the right ones, no one can tell how this war will end. Now even the Americans believe that there will be neither victors nor vanquished in this war. No one who has seen this operation at first hand can fail to realise that what is happening is something totally new, something really revolutionary.

The American tiger which is poised to attack in Vietnam is not made of paper. Its teeth and claws are as hard as steel. But this tiger's mind is not just a military mind and its heart-beat is not only attuned to the rhythm of the armaments industry. This book is about that tiger, which the Chinese communists still say is made of paper.

2

'LADIES and gentlemen, in a few minutes we shall be landing at Saigon airport. Would you kindly fasten your seat-belts and refrain from smoking.'

The usual announcement from the loudspeaker of the Boeing 707, as though we were about to land at any airport in a friendly world. But the 'few minutes' in which we were to have landed at Saigon airport became an hour and forty minutes. For that length of time we circled in the monsoon clouds over Saigon.

It wasn't the weather which prevented our landing. Each time there was a brief break in the clouds I could see why we had not yet been allowed to land: behind us in the sky trailed no less than twenty-eight other aircraft. And the number was increasing. Enormous three-decker transport planes, probably packed with troops and ammunition. Saigon airport kept coming into view: the runway looked like an ant track. While the heavy transport planes were landing, double rows of jet bombers loaded with rockets shot from the other end of the runway like arrows into the sky. We were in the midst of an air-lift operation, and not just one, but probably two, three or four of them. On the aircraft circling round with us I could clearly read: 'United States Army', 'United States Air Force', 'Military Air Transport System', 'USOM', 'United States Navy'.

At last, after nearly two hours of waiting, our machine—an aeroplane belonging to one of the major international airlines—was given permission to land. We landed on the runway only a hundred yards behind a heavy US transport plane, and as our Boeing taxied towards the hangars, two more aircraft had already landed behind us.

Several days later I was looking around the control tower of Saigon airport. The radar screen which registers the arrival and departure of aircraft made my hair stand on end: many hundreds of take-offs and landings are scheduled daily at this airport.

As we taxied towards the airport buildings we had our first glimpse of the war. The tarmac was crammed with jet fighters, jet bombers, transport machines, reconnaissance aircraft, meteorological aircraft and literally hundreds of helicopters. Between them were endless columns of ammunition trucks bringing bombs, rockets and shells for the cannon of the fighter planes. Sandbag barricades had been erected around this area and high concrete walls round the huge bombers. South Vietnamese and American sentries in steel helmets and bullet-proof jackets, rifles or machine-pistols at the ready, stood guarding the barricades. This is just one of many airfields in South Vietnam, and one which is, furthermore, open to civilian traffic.

Even in these first few minutes I could see something of the scale of the war effort in Vietnam. But there was to be another surprise: as we left our aircraft, there, waiting for us at the bottom of the gang-way, were charming Vietnamese stewardesses wearing long white silk trousers and the characteristically Vietnamese tunics with deep side-slits of turquoise blue. 'Welcome to Vietnam,' they said to each passenger with an enchanting smile. Was *this* war?

I prepared myself for strict passport and baggage control, for complications and for hours of waiting. Next surprise: the immigration officer, who spoke fluent French, merely glanced at my passport and the customs official dealt with my luggage in a second. No questions. No checks. But I was not the only one to be treated like this. The incoming Vietnamese, too, sailed through the arrival procedure, and at the airport exit the taxi-drivers were busily fighting over passengers.

I looked back again at the vast waiting hall. One announcement caught my eye: between the 'Air France' and 'Air Vietnam' counters hung a sign over another similar checking-in counter: 'United States Air Force'. A perfectly ordinary counter at which American pilots were queuing like the civilians near by.

From then on until the end of my stay in Vietnam, I had again and again to get used to the fact that the war in Vietnam is only an 'interpolation': that throughout South Vietnam there are these two interlocking campaigns—war and peace.

This was equally clear from a glance at the streets through which I travelled in the centre of Saigon. It was rush hour, and interminable streams of traffic were on the move as in any European capital: hundreds of taxis and cars, thousands of motor-cycles, scooters, mopeds as well as the bicycles and tri-shaws which are both so popular here. The pavements, too, were thronged with people—the sort of dense crowd which is only to be found in overpopulated Asia.

It was 90 degrees in the shade and the humidity touched 100 per cent, yet everyone was scurrying at top speed—gesticulating street vendors, milling pedestrians pushing each other along past hundreds of shop windows; cars, scooters and bicycles trying to overtake one another in the six lanes of traffic amid much hooting and bell-ringing. At each crossroads half a dozen policemen attempted with partial success to control some of the converging traffic.

And yet there was a war on. In the midst of the mass of little Renault taxis, jeeps and trucks of the Vietnamese and American armies were constantly seen, and the patrol cars of the military police, the 'Three in a Jeep' as I was soon to call them because they were each occupied by a white American, an American Negro and a South Vietnamese, were everywhere.

There were also a number of buildings which the pedestrian was forced to bypass. They were surrounded by dozens of large white concrete blocks laced with barbed wire and guarded by policemen in white uniforms with sub-machine-guns at the ready, and Vietnamese or American soldiers with fixed bayonets. These were government buildings, staff quarters, military hospitals, rest centres for officers and men, police stations, ministries—and the American Embassy which had been severely bombed only a few months earlier. To get to it you have to go through a small maze of controls and barricades which resemble 'Check Point Charlie' in Berlin.

But the eye quickly gets used to all this. Barbed wire and machine-guns cannot alter the fundamentally peaceful character of this city, which was once called the Paris of the Far East and whose atmosphere today is still an enchanting mixture of Paris and the Orient. If the Vietcong wanted to strike here, it would be easy for them. How can any authority hope to keep a check on the two million inhabitants of Saigon? Who can illumine the million corners of the thousands of shops and the cramped, overcrowded flats and homes of two million people who live packed together in the narrow confines of this city?

12

The police therefore concentrate on checking the incoming roads, the bridges and the river bank of the Mekong by night, as they have never been fully successful in making this temperamental people observe even the brief curfew from midnight until four a.m.

It was evening when my taxi turned into the notorious market-place of Saigon. Here students and Buddhists gather before starting their massive protest marches. This is where tear-gas is used and where the police shoot to kill.

That evening there was no sign of any of this. The stalls in the market were overflowing with fruit and vegetables and with such oriental specialities as octopus, roasted locusts and the many exotic delicacies which are presented to you steaming hot on banana leaves. Up above, in a flood of coloured neon lighting, branded products from all over the world and a dozen new films from America, France and Japan were advertised. Naturally all these visual impressions were strongly emphasised by the thousand smells of Asia, the shouting of street vendors and the cacophony of motor horns.

The better hotels of the town lie to the left and right of the Opera House along the Rue Catinat. I stayed at the Continental Palace, where two policemen were on permanent duty at the entrance. There are policemen armed with rifles or pistols outside every hotel for foreigners. Some time ago all the restaurants and bars in Saigon had steel lattice put over their windows so that the Vietcong would not be able to toss in bombs as they drove by. The Continental Palace is the only place where the bar terrace on the street level has no grating or protection. Large fans attached to the ceiling blow cool air over the guests. Later on I discovered why they were so 'careless' here: the Polish members of the International Commission for Vietnam live in this hotel and they therefore consider themselves safe from Vietcong attack.

The hotel porter offered me a brochure entitled 'What's new in Saigon?' This was exactly what I wanted to find out, but I didn't find anything in it that I had expected. It is a weekly publication advertising the night-club programmes, the names of the bars, the variety theatres, the cinema and theatre programmes, the galleries and exhibitions. There were also, ironically enough, invitations to go shooting:

13

elephants, tigers and leopards could be hunted. The major car firms also advertised: 'Buy your car here, tax and duty free. It is waiting for you ready to drive on your return to the USA.'

Another slogan caught my attention: 'Relax in perfect safety in our restaurant (in our bar, in our hotel).' Perfect safety—Saigon's catchphrase. Too often restaurants, bars, cinemas and other places of entertainment have been attacked by Vietcong bombs.

And it soon became clear why this slogan is so important: these hotels and restaurants are not only occupied by business people, travellers and journalists. Wherever one goes one meets soldiers and officers of the allied forces who are staying in them, too, men just back from the front line who book a modern, air-conditioned hotel room, slip out of their stained uniform and put on a white shirt and a light tropical suit. Three hours after leaving the jungle they are being served with a whisky and soda by a pretty Vietnamese barmaid. For them perfect safety is of even greater importance, because it is perhaps their first leave after weeks of fighting.

After dusk there are the ubiquitous lanky Americans with little Vietnamese girlfriends who reach no higher than their armpits. The bars, which used to have predominantly French names, have been re-styled to suit the customers. You can now find places called 'Johnny', 'San Francisco', 'Miami', 'The Golden Coast' and whatever other American names they can think of. In fact it is easy to get the impression that the only danger for a white man in the streets of Saigon is the horde of people who accost you at every turn, trying to interest you in all kinds of deals.

First and foremost they want to buy black market American dollars (on the black market they are rated at a third above the official exchange), and they offer to help you pass the night in 'safe' female company. On the walls of the houses in front of which these types do business are enormous placards—'Stop the black market! Get rid of smugglers and war profiteers!' On these posters a strong fist clutches a tout by the scruff of the neck and dollar bills are pouring out of his coat pockets.

The strong hand operates, moreover, by night on the streets of Saigon: Vietnamese police patrols, small and lithe, are at work rapidly frisking passers-by who have been detained. In their midst stroll the six-feet-tall American military police keeping a keen eye on off-duty

GIs. It is mainly thanks to these patrols that this city, which was once nicknamed 'A Thousand Vices', now leads, in spite of everything, a more or less orderly existence.

At twenty minutes to midnight, however, there is suddenly more bustle than is ever seen by day in Saigon. It is closing time for the many restaurants and bistros, night-clubs and bars, and the hundreds of nightbirds call for taxis and tri-shaws to speed them home before the curfew begins. This is also the time when many citizens of Saigon pack up their little charcoal braziers on the banks of the Mekong river and hurry back home. As a matter of course in the hot, heavy monsoon season they prefer the cool of the river down by the docks during the evening and buy dried fish from the street vendors to grill on their own stoves.

If you open one of the twenty-three Vietnamese daily papers, or one of the two English-language newspapers, in Saigon and find the main interest revolving around the attractive new uniforms for the women police, you can be almost convinced that peace reigns in Vietnam.

But appearances are deceptive—at times violently so. There are nights when several bombs explode simultaneously in the city and days when 'policemen' masquerading in stolen uniforms drive into police stations and blow a jeep full of plastic explosive sky high.

Anyone who cares to let his gaze wander from the sixth-floor bar of the Majestic Hotel, disregarding the music and the sweet voice of the Vietnamese singer, is forced to think again about this 'peace' when he looks over the Mekong river. No more than five or six kilometres beyond the river a battle rages, gunfire flashes, tracer bullets blaze from aircraft cannon. Searchlights illuminate the opposite river bank and you can picture the government troops fighting off a Vietcong mortar attack on the town.

You can follow the war in Vietnam, if you wish, from the terrace of your hotel, whisky glass in hand. But the rattle of machine-guns is drowned by the noisy activity of the streets and the shellbursts are muffled by the loud whirring of the ventilating system. Only now and then do the window panes in the houses of Saigon start to rattle: this is when the bombers of the US Strategic Air Force Command are on their way to Vietcong territory, eight-jet supersonic bombers which unload hundreds of tons of conventional bombs over the jungle—fifteen, twenty, perhaps twenty-five miles outside Saigon. And the whole town rocks.

When this roar of jet engines almost shot me out of bed on my first night in Saigon, I quickly turned on the radio. An air raid? No need to worry; there is no blackout nor do they anticipate an enemy air attack. The trenches which were once dug in Saigon's parks have long since been covered with refuse or filled in with mud by the heavy tropical rains. The American Forces network in Vietnam, which I had just turned on to find out whether danger was imminent, was broadcasting the latest hit songs from the States. Between the numbers there came the soft, girlish voice of the announcer: 'This is your foxholemate Betsy, East of Midnight. How are you today?'

Yes, that's what I wanted to know. How were the Vietnamese and American soldiers out there where the flames in the night sky prove that peace does not reign over this country? I was to find out soon enough.

3

At six o'clock in the morning we took off from Saigon Airport. Our target was a little town on the east coast of Vietnam, one and a half hours' flying time away over the jungle-covered mountains. One and a half hours during which the pilot repeatedly pointed his forefinger at the ground to indicate that we were over Vietcong territory.

I had been briefed exactly as to what I had to do if the aircraft was hit or shot down. I had signed a form saying that I and my relatives renounced any right to compensation from the USA or from the South Vietnamese Government if I were wounded or killed. I had given precise details on another form as to who should be informed in case I did not return from this flight. And I had left three photographs in the desk drawer of a master-sergeant to facilitate identification 'if necessary'.

I had also examined with interest the emergency kit issued to American airmen flying over Vietnam: parachute and reserve parachute, two-way transmitter, pistol, Very pistol, bush-knife, solid fuel methylated spirits and cooker, dinghy and a nylon sheet to serve as sail, rainwater catchment and protection against tropical storms, complete fishing tackle, a mirror (for signalling passing aircraft), a compass and ordnance survey maps of all territories. There was, of course, a small transistor radio and a piece of material marked with the sentence: 'Please give me something to eat' in many languages and dialects.

The most fascinating however was a 'card game'. There were cards which showed in detail every plant, fruit, root and animal which it was safe to eat in the jungle or out at sea. There was also a first-aid box with anti-malarial pills, anti-insect ointment, bandages—and a little bag of shark-repellent chemicals.

'We won't need any of that,' said the pilot reassuringly.

I hoped he was right, but it wasn't a pleasant feeling to be flying only a few hundred feet above the mountain tops which were marked Vietcong territory on our maps. In the event, everything went as smoothly as a flip over the Alps. It was only when a wide runway became visible beneath us and the pilot was preparing to land that I grew doubtful. This landing strip was not only on the edge of the jungle, it was completely deserted; there was not a single aircraft or car near the huts on the edge of the runway. Stranger still, not a sentry was to be seen. Were things really so quiet here? The pilot also found it odd. He was trying in vain to get in touch with the airfield on the radio, but either we were on the wrong wavelength or the aerodrome wasn't answering. We circled once, twice, three times around the deserted runway. Not a soul to be seen. The pilot checked and rechecked his flight instructions with base. 'That's it,' he said. 'That's landing strip number 17. This is where we're supposed to land.' Those were our instructions.

It all looked too odd for comfort, so we climbed in a wide circle away from the airfield in the direction of the village about ten kilometres away. There things looked different. The streets were packed with military vehicles and soldiers, and in the middle of the village we discovered a little emergency airfield, a runway made out of metal strips. Near the runway there were aircraft and helicopters. 'That's where we'll land,' said the pilot.

As we were preparing to land, we could already see figures on the edge of the airport waving excitedly, and as we got out of the plane they greeted us with the words: 'Thank God you came down here. We were worried that you might land on number 17. Number 17 is now within the range of Vietcong artillery.'

We were in an 'insecure area', so called because a large part of it is under Vietcong control. The Vietcong are here in such strength that they can attack at any time and be sure of success. This is an area in which there is not yet a single US Army unit. South Vietnamese government troops operate here. They can do no more than protect the ricefields on the plains and in the valleys and guard the capital of the province and the surrounding villages. At the moment they have ninety American 'advisers'. An 'adviser' can be many things: an NCO who advises a South Vietnamese platoon commander, or a colonel who discusses operations with South Vietnamese staff officers.

Here the ninety American advisers were soldiers ranking from corporal to major. I was soon to get to know many of them. They had come with a column of heavily armoured jeeps to collect me. We drove past anti-aircraft guns, barbed wire fences, look-out towers and concrete bunkers on our way to the military camp on the coast. 'The helicopters will soon be here,' said the American captain who was driving my jeep, and added: 'You've arrived just in time to see our counter-attack.'

In the square in front of the long barracks the South Vietnamese troops were getting ready for action: small, sinewy, dressed in paratroops' camouflage suits, hung with rifles, machine-guns and hand grenades, with cartridge belts worn crosswise over their chests. None of them was taller than five and a half feet. Leading each section were four American soldiers or NCOs, each of them over six feet tall. Orders rang out, there was a rattle of rifle-bolts and magazines were swiftly loaded. With the Americans in the lead, the troops marched off in step, but they soon broke ranks. At the edge of the ricefields, between the bamboos and where the jungle reaches the outskirts of the town, they disappeared into thin air. 'We don't march in ranks,' explained the captain who was accompanying me. 'Here, on this exact spot, the French lost a whole regiment because they were marching in step and in strict formation.'

As we tried to keep up with the troops I had my first lesson in partisan warfare. 'First of all,' I was told, 'the most important thing: the Vietcongs are only human. Besides being badly trained they are poorly armed and underfed. Therefore they can be beaten. On the other hand, they are brave and they have one advantage which we don't have—they can attack where and when they want, and they can run away and go to ground after an attack. Our disadvantage is that we have to find them. Often their main object is not to cause us heavy losses; that wouldn't be a bad thing for us because then they would have to operate in full strength.

'The Vietcong are out to intimidate the population, to show them that they are never far away and will always reappear and that no one can be sure of his life if he co-operates with the government. The most dangerous job in this province is to be mayor of a village. One mayor after another gets killed off by the Vietcong.'

I asked why. The American captain had been here for a year. His short laugh showed that he considered my question naive. 'Why!' he repeated. 'The Vietcong need three things: rice, money and recruits. They get these three things from the people and to do so they must keep them subservient. There was a time when the communists tried to do this by persuasion, by being friendly and helping the population. This is no longer so.

'The Vietcong are short of time, they lack trained cadres and above all they no longer possess the conviction of victory as a psychological weapon: 80 per cent of this province is controlled by the Vietcong. This is both true and untrue. We would say with equal justification that we control 80 per cent. The Vietcong is everywhere and nowhere. And so are we—everywhere and nowhere.'

During the next two days I was able to confirm that this curious statement was no exaggeration. The Americans, of whom it was once said that they would only dig in along the coastline and would simply try to hold the main towns, have given up these tactics. 'We never intended to use these methods,' I was told later at a staff H.Q. 'But we needed time in the beginning so that we could at least get our troops ready. Now we are up to fighting strength. Now we deploy our units in exactly the same tactical fashion as the Vietcong themselves.'

Take, for example, the American 1st Cavalry Division. Nowadays instead of horses they ride helicopters and this division is using over 400 of these aircraft in Vietnam. They fly through the monsoon clouds in formation, as the cavalry brigades once galloped across the battlefield, and true to tradition they charge the enemy from the flank and attack him from the rear. There is no territory in South Vietnam where they cannot operate. Their commanders purposely look for territory where neither French nor Vietnamese government troops have set foot in the last twenty years, jungle and mountain territory in which the Vietcong have, up to now, felt completely safe.

'We often don't know ourselves what we'll find there,' I was told. 'Sometimes nothing, but sometimes our people land in the middle of the headquarters of a Vietcong regiment.'

At first correspondents in Vietnam smiled at these 'negative' American operations. They no longer smile. Even when the American attacks were only being carried out at half strength, there were more than a thousand deserters a month from the ranks of the Vietcong. These deserters were starving and in a state of shock. They all said the same thing: the non-stop air attacks were wrecking the morale of the Vietcong. At least one result of the American intrusion tactics was that there was nowhere safe left for the Vietcong to withdraw to and rest.

The Vietcong are in retreat. They may still be able to assemble in battalion strength and can still succeed in laying ambushes and destroying weak units of government or American troops. But the Vietcong, who had previously been operating from totally secure bases, have no safe bases any longer.

Their supplies are also dwindling. The American bombing raids on the North Vietnamese supply routes are beginning to have their effect in the South. They need weapons. They need food supplies. They need experienced leaders and officers. This emerges as an indisputable fact when one talks to deserters and prisoners. That is why the Vietcong are now trying all the harder to prove that they are still intact and still capable of attack. They occasionally take a big gamble in order to achieve a small but psychologically important victory somewhere.

'Their most effective method for this is still for pockets of Vietcong to slip through our lines at night carrying one or two grenades with them and to open fire at close quarters on our airfields,' explained the captain. 'These men are as brave as lions—you could almost compare them with the Japanese Kamikaze pilots in the Second World War. But from a military standpoint their attacks count for nothing. Material losses hardly matter in our army.'

But the Vietcong still succeed in surrounding distant outposts manned by Vietnamese government troops, which they overrun, usually with heavy losses. 'This is already a considerable change, in comparison with the earlier Vietcong tactics,' the captain pointed out. 'The Vietcong used to conserve their manpower. They never attacked when there would be heavy losses, but now it is a matter of winning at any price. If you ask me it's a clear case of desperation.'

These methods, moreover, do not make it any easier for the Americans. In this sort of fighting the honour of the Vietnamese government troops is at stake. On the whole they try to hold their ground on their own. Although they accept American air force support, they refuse the assistance of American ground troops. Since there is no joint American-

Vietnamese supreme command, the Americans can only step in when South Vietnam asks them for help. Thus there are still heavy losses of government troops where this should no longer be necessary.

One example was the battle of Plei Me. Apparently in this case the Americans were only called in when the South Vietnamese reserve troops being brought up for Plei Me were pinned down in the jungle. Again it was the 1st American Cavalry Division which stepped in and decided the battle in a matter of hours.

'But don't think we underestimate the Vietcong,' the captain went on. 'In this country of impenetrable jungle and mountains the Vietcong have every chance of slipping out of our grasp.' Nevertheless the captain was not only convinced that the Vietcong are in a poor military condition but also that their morale has been fatally weakened.

'It is significant that the Vietcong are even abandoning their dead. We know from statements made by prisoners, confirmed by actual evidence, that the Vietcong have orders first and foremost to secure the weapons and the rice sacks. They leave the dead where they fall.'

'I don't see anything extraordinary in leaving the dead to the enemy,' I said.

'Oh yes, it is something very unusual,' asserted the South Vietnamese major who was travelling with us. 'It is very hard to enlist recruits in Vietnam unless you can convince them and their families that, should they fall, they will be buried with full ceremonial honours. This is part of the belief in honouring their ancestors, which is deep-rooted in Vietnam. Death does not seem so fearful once it is certain that the members of the family and future generations can honour the dead man at his grave. It is terrible not to know where a dead man is buried. And this presents the Vietcong with great recruiting difficulties. Those who don't bring back the dead will not be entrusted with the living,' explained the major.

All this has contributed to the fact that the Vietcong are beginning to lose one of their best weapons: their political objective. Their policy was aimed at winning over the South Vietnamese population and ensuring their loyal backing for the Vietcong, but as soon as the Vietcong are on the run they no longer have the time or the resources to consider the feelings of the people. They demand rice, money and recruits, and they are demanding them with growing desperation—all

the rice, all the money and all the young people, girls as well as boys—
without bringing back the dead.

That afternoon government troops recaptured airfield number 17.
The Vietcong had vanished. Our troops pushed deep into the jungle.
I marched with them from village to village. We exchanged shots with
snipers. In some villages we were received with fear and mistrust. In
others the children called out to us and the adults smiled timidly.

'Neither side is greeted as a liberator nowadays. Today we are here;
yesterday it was the Vietcong. These people live in permanent fear.
Fear of both sides.'

I talked to many villagers during this march. They only wanted one
thing: that the war should end. Of course they all asserted that the
government must win the war. They were all against the Vietcong.
But I could well imagine what answers they had given the Vietcong
to the same questions the day before. . . .

Can the war be won? By either side? And how can it be done?

The troops on the spot tried to answer these questions for me. Two
days later in Saigon I was shown detailed plans of how this objective
might be achieved.

4

In the centre of Saigon there is a modern building, several stories high, barricaded with cement blocks and barbed wire and guarded by Vietnamese police and American military police. Anyone who enters the building has to identify himself with a pass, complete with photograph, authorised by the organisation operating here.

Even the American love of abbreviations is hard put to it to simplify the name of this organisation. It is called 'JUSPAO', which is short for Joint United States Public Affairs Operation. It would be far more accurate if it were simply named 'Mission for Psychological Warfare'. It is a mammoth organisation and was created at the personal wish of President Johnson. It is called 'Joint' because it puts experts of widely differing American organisations side by side—journalists and broadcasters, economists and sociologists, public relations officers of all three American forces, diplomats and political advisers.

Only the headquarters of JUSPAO is in Saigon. Branch offices are found wherever there are American units stationed in South Vietnam and wherever the South Vietnamese government exerts the slightest influence. This organisation has taken on an apparently superhuman task. And only time will tell whether the Americans succeed in achieving the impossible. For the aim of JUSPAO, and other American organisations, is nothing less than to help the South Vietnamese to overcome the accumulated disasters of 3,000 years of troubled history—centuries of oppression, internecine warfare, religious divisions, local dictators, foreign colonial rule, corruption and the disintegration of society. In the circumstances JUSPAO's biggest problem is how to make it clear to the South Vietnamese that these activities are serving the interests of South Vietnam and not those of the USA.

'We have learnt,' one of the senior officials of JUSPAO explained

24

to me. 'We Americans used to believe that the world could only be happy by adopting our standards. What's good for America must be good for everybody. We believed you could teach democracy and a free enterprise system to other people, that we had a *mission* to do so. Haven't we tried to force our way of life on other nations once too often?'

I was astonished to hear such frankness. But what are the consequences to be drawn from this self-criticism? The answer to this question took almost a whole hour. Here are the most important points:

The best defence a nation can have against a forcible takeover by communism is a sense of national identity and a pride in its own way of life.

It would therefore be completely wrong to attempt to 'sell' a foreign political philosophy along with a supply of weapons as a package deal to any country fighting communism.

If a nation wants help, then it should be limited to providing material and moral aid for its own chosen projects.

The recipients should feel that they can say 'no' at any time, that they can break their links with the donor and that they alone control the present and future use of the aid.

All aid should have a single goal—to strengthen the country's own sense of national identity.

The first task of the new American team, which had only recently begun to operate this programme in South Vietnam, was to convince the government and the South Vietnamese army that these principles really were fundamental to US policy towards Vietnam.

'This wasn't easy,' said my companion, 'because there are too many politicians and officials in South Vietnam who have never heard of such an approach and never experienced anything like it. For centuries foreign rulers and colonial officers governed this country and prescribed to the puppet government and hired civil servants exactly what they were to do and not do.

'Even communism as it is now practised in North Vietnam has only partially contributed towards a sense of national identity and purpose. It introduced ideas which were alien to the Vietnamese people and which to some extent they have still not assimilated.

'In this way, our own principles often turn out to be traps for ourselves. We have to deal with senior South Vietnamese government officials and we always find that they expect us to carry out and administer the projects ourselves, yet that is just what we want to avoid. We are ready to provide money, material, ideas, organisational techniques and a small army of advisers, but the administrators must be South Vietnamese and furthermore they must know what they want and what they don't want.'

The first and simplest measure which the Americans have taken as an essential psychological adjunct to their programme has been the strictest adherence to protocol. I have seen high-ranking American officers in Vietnam standing to attention in front of South Vietnamese army officers saying: 'Yes, Major,' 'Very good, Colonel.' This respect for the rank of South Vietnamese officials extends beyond the purely military level. No American press officer was prepared to receive me before I had been acknowledged by the South Vietnamese government as a journalist. Only when I could show my South Vietnamese press card to the American authorities was I given an American pass, which specifically quoted the serial number of my Vietnamese accreditation card.

No American reception, no celebration, no handing-over of material aid, no presentation of money ever takes place without top South Vietnamese officials in the place of honour, often one step in front of the American ambassador or the American general.

Although I shall return to this point in greater detail later, I should mention here that it is just this attitude of the Americans which made it so easy for the South Vietnamese to overthrow their own governments again and again. Contrary to their earlier practice (i.e. when Prime Minister Diem was in power) the Americans now avoid involvement in the South Vietnamese internal political power game.

'We help each South Vietnamese government which wants help,' says JUSPAO. 'We have no personal alliance with any politician, any military official, any church leader. Home affairs are without exception left to the South Vietnamese.'

American policy in South Vietnam is beset with a number of dangers. The first and most obvious is the potential (and actual) corruption and misappropriation of aid. The Americans are helpless when a provincial governor or a mayor channels off a large portion of American aid and does not apply it to its proper end. American advisers operating in the provinces on the edge of the Vietcong areas are seriously worried by this problem.

The second danger is that a political *coup* could install overnight a government which might throw the Americans out altogether, along with their troops and their aid. 'Then there would be nothing for us but to leave the country,' they explained at JUSPAO, although I find it hard to believe that this would actually happen.

Thirdly, in spite of all their good intentions, the presence of so many American soldiers may arouse feelings of dislike, antagonism and in the end, hatred.

At the moment there is little danger of this to be seen in Vietnam. Quite apart from the very generous American financial and economic aid to Vietnam, every single American soldier is also an extraordinary source of profit for many Vietnamese.

When one realises that the monthly income of a Vietnamese peasant or even an office worker is between 8 and 15 dollars and that the American soldiers are prepared to spend 100 to 200 dollars a month on drink, souvenirs, necessities and every kind of amusement, that some hundred thousand American soldiers are stationed in Vietnam, one can see why every man in uniform holds a special attraction for the Vietnamese.

The GIs are thus, as I could see for myself, still welcome. And one of the most natural sights in Saigon is to see these soldiers walking through the town hand in hand with half a dozen children. There is something in it for everyone.

In Europe the relatively high pay of the American soldier has often provoked envy and antipathy. In a country like Vietnam where the economy is so underdeveloped, where the population has not so much as dreamed of reaching the foreigners' standard of living, this feeling is not yet obvious, but JUSPAO is very aware of the danger and tries to steer clear of it.

On the day I arrived in Saigon, the English-language newspapers gave prominent coverage to an order issued by the US Commander-in-Chief in Vietnam, General Westmoreland. This order to all American troops ran as follows:

1. Remember we are guests here: We make no demands and seek no special treatment.
2. Join with the people! Understand their life, use phrases from their language and honor their customs and laws.
3. Treat women with politeness and respect.
4. Make personal friends among the soldiers and common people.
5. Always give the Vietnamese the right of way.
6. Be alert to security and ready to react with your military skill.
7. Don't attract attention by loud, rude or unusual behavior.
8. Avoid separating yourself from the people by a display of wealth or privilege.
9. Above all you are members of the US Military Forces on a difficult mission, responsible for all your official and personal actions. Reflect honor upon yourself and the United States of America.

On the day of publication General Westmoreland's nine commandments (drafted by JUSPAO) were issued on a handy, plastic-covered card to every American soldier. 'It looks like an identity card and it is an identity card,' it was explained to me. The military police have been ordered to check continually that these plastic cards with the 'Nine Rules for Personnel of US Military Assistance Command, Vietnam' are always carried by every GI.

This standing order reminded me of Mao Tse-tung's action at the beginning of his war for the 'hearts and minds' of the Chinese people in 1927, when he issued three rules and nine commandments for the Red Army soldiers. The majority of General Westmoreland's orders are practically identical with them.

5

JUSPAO headquarters in Saigon does not classify its activities in any order of priority. Everything is of equal importance, whether it is the provision of detailed Press information to the outside world on everything that happens in Vietnam or the morale of each and every village controlled by the American or Vietnamese government troops. Although I had already seen both American diplomacy and the American army at work in many other parts of the world, I found that JUSPAO had initiated some very surprising innovations in Vietnam.

We were once again in Vietcong territory, in a small Vietnamese village about twenty-five kilometres outside a provincial capital. Our column of armoured jeeps had approached this village with extreme caution, as the Vietcong were known to have mined the verges of these narrow paths. The troops escorting us held their rifles and pistols at the ready in order to react immediately to a Vietcong ambush.

I was therefore all the more surprised when we arrived in the village. In the middle of the village street stood a solitary American civilian. He was wearing cotton drill trousers, bush-shirt and a heavy pistol in his belt. He smiled and waved at us. I was introduced to him. He was a political officer although he was simply called an 'adviser'.

The American troops referred to his house as 'The Embassy', for the very good reason that the man was a trained diplomat: he was political adviser to the Vietnamese provincial governor. Among his many other duties he was also particularly concerned with establishing contact with the local population. It was he who had set up the political administration in this village. He discussed the needs and problems of the village with the inhabitants, encouraged them to elect a mayor and helped the mayor to set up a village council drawn from their own ranks.

Apart from this he also had a special duty. Suddenly within the space of a few minutes young Vietnamese in black uniforms appeared from the bushes and hedges and from the bamboo groves. Every one of them was armed to the teeth: pistols in their belts, hand grenades on shoulder-straps, light and heavy machine-guns, rifles and machine-pistols.

'Those are our PATs,' I was told. PAT stands for 'Political Action Team'.

'Who are they?' I asked.

'Most of them are former members of the Vietcong,' replied the JUSPAO man blandly.

They were young men of the village, who not long ago had been recruited by the Vietcong and who had fought in the ranks of the Vietcong. They deserted partly of their own free will and partly as a result of JUSPAO's psychological warfare, surrendering voluntarily and often with their weapons in their hands to the Vietnamese government troops or to the Americans.

'These are the best,' explained the JUSPAO man, 'because they know the Vietcong—not just their battle tactics but also the way they recruit and the way they treat the population. They don't necessarily disagree with these methods—in fact they believe that the Vietcong were right in much of what they did. What they didn't like was the growing harshness of the system. They may have felt, too, that they were on the losing side with the Vietcong. Besides, and this should not be underestimated, they wanted to be with their parents, wives and children. The Vietcong had originally promised them that they could stay in their village, but they had been unable to keep this promise.'

The Americans formed these deserters into units and the men were then sent to political rehabilitation camps. There the distinction between the Vietcong and the government was drilled into them by South Vietnamese officials with American advisers. 'The idea of democracy doesn't make much impression on these people,' said my informant. 'Firstly, they can hardly imagine what it means. Secondly, conditions are still far from democratic in South Vietnam. But certain ideas have an immediate impact on them: individual rights, humanity, sympathy, respect for family life, law, love—to name but a few. But don't misunderstand me; there was a time when the government army fell a long way short of these ideals and in some regions it still does, perhaps understandably, after so many years of hard and brutal fighting. However, the present government is making an effort to instil these ideas into its troops and to conduct the war, on practical as well as on psychological grounds, on our lines. Part of this programme is here in front of you.'

The JUSPAO official pointed in the direction of the heavily armed black-uniformed soldiers.

After the political rehabilitation (when I jokingly mentioned the word 'brainwashing', they agreed with me) the deserters are retrained with modern American weapons and, above all, in a new method of warfare.

'We don't want the PATs to fight the Vietcong,' the JUSPAO man went on. 'We want to avoid the risk of putting too much of a strain on their loyalties, because many of them still have links with Vietcong leaders. Our goal is different. We give these people precisely what the Vietcong promised them, but failed to provide: the chance to stay with their families. We make the protection of their families their own responsibility. They should, moreover, be able to lead their lives in their villages just as they had imagined and as they had originally hoped they would under the Vietcong: a democratic village adminis-tration—without having to use the word democracy or the abstract rules of democracy.

'It is simply a matter of electing the mayor and the officials from the people they trust most within the village community. It is also a question of an equitable distribution of land so that everyone who works a patch of ground should also own it. It includes building a school for the children and a clinic for the whole community. It is important that they should be able to harvest the rice in safety and take it just as safely to town to be sold. They need drinking water laid on by pipe lines—all the things, in fact, which they have so far never had, all the things which the Vietcong promised them in theory and for which they accepted the Vietcong.

'The aim of USOM [United States Operational Mission] is to make this possible. The PATs are only supposed to prepare the political ground for us, to remind the villagers every day that our side, the side of the South Vietnamese government, really achieves something where the Vietcong only made promises. Apart from all this the PATs are meant to protect the village, and for the first time they have something which they really want to protect.'

I spoke to various members of this Political Action Team. Their notions are simple, but effective: 'We don't want the Vietcong to come back and take our property away,' said one of them. 'We don't want the Vietcong to confiscate our rice,' declared another. 'We want to stay with our families,' explained a third.

These soldiers have put up thick barbed wire around their village, they have erected watch-towers and they lie in wait at night in ambush. They know how the Vietcong generally attack a village and their patrols therefore spread out far afield. They quietly let the small Vietcong raiding parties pass them by, only to attack from the rear as soon as they are forced to stand and fight along the barbed-wire barricade.

When conditions permit, the PATs move from village to village performing little plays and musical sketches, all with a political slant—government is good, Vietcong is bad—and they talk to the people of other villages and try to convince them in their own simple words.

'But don't imagine that the establishment of the PATs has turned the tide, or has had much military effect at all on this campaign,' I was told. 'We are only at the start of this programme and it will only be successful if the whole military situation continues to develop in our favour. The setting up of the PATs is just one of several means we are now trying to use in order to win the "hearts and minds" of the people for the Government.'

There have inevitably been informers and traitors among the PATs. It has also happened that the regular government troops have used the same coercive methods to recruit PAT members for the front line that the Vietcong used before them. 'Unfortunately there are still officers in the regular army who don't understand the aims and objectives of the PATs and simply take the well-armed and well-trained PATs with them to fill up their battalions, so we have to send these officers on training course to make it clear to them why they should leave the PATs alone. In time we shall succeed.'

Thus the PAT programme has its setbacks. An important step was taken during my stay in Vietnam, when the PATs were made the direct responsibility of the Americans 'at the request of the South Vietnamese government'.

Along with the PATs, another project is being put into operation. It is potentially far more effective, although it too has its pitfalls. In Vietnamese this programme is called 'Chiu Hoi', meaning in English 'Open Arms'. Its objective is obvious from its name—to induce the Vietcong to desert and to receive the deserters 'with open arms'. This idea was also developed by the Americans but met with considerable opposition from the South Vietnamese troop commanders. Finally it was accepted by the government as desirable and is slowly taking shape.

The 'Chiu Hoi' scheme is a complex operation. First the members of the Vietcong have to be informed that the plan exists, that they can desert without danger and that they will be received by the government 'with open arms'. Helicopters with loudspeakers fly over Vietcong territory announcing the aims and objectives of the programme. Other aeroplanes drop leaflets over Vietcong territory with the same message. Government troops and Americans post notices on trees on their patrols through the jungle, urging the Vietcong to desert.

'But there is nothing so effective as word of mouth,' I was told at JUSPAO. 'It is incredible what can and does filter through into the ranks of the Vietcong.'

Members of the Vietcong are told the following:

Deserters will be well treated.

Those who bring their weapons with them will get a large reward for each weapon. (This serves to induce the Vietcong to bring in arms, which are hard to replace. The Vietcong also offers the government troops high rewards for weapons, but they often fail to pay due to lack of funds.)

Anyone who deserts—even without weapons—will immediately be given two suits of clothes. He will also get a daily rate of pay equivalent to that of a South Vietnamese soldier, which ensures that he is well fed.

Each deserter then has to attend a three- to six-week political rehabilitation course.

If he can return to his family, i.e., providing they live in one of the government-controlled areas, he will not only be repatriated but will be given a resettlement bounty, generally about two months' pay, together with seed, clothes for the family, furniture and other concessions.

When he feels ready for it, he will be incorporated into the PAT in his own village.

If he cannot return to his family because his home is in Vietcong territory, then he can do one of two things: he can either join any family he knows and live with them—and in view of the material aid which each deserter gets he is welcome in many families—or he can have a piece of land to cultivate. In this case efforts are made—again by word of mouth—to get his family out of Vietcong territory. This works in an astonishing number of cases.

The deserter can, if he wishes, enter a government training camp where he learns a new trade. Later, a suitable job is found for him, usually in one of the towns.

It caused the Americans considerable trouble to set up this programme. They could only act as long as they had the co-operation of the government, who like most Asiatics are disinclined to show much sympathy for 'the enemy'. Government troops hate the Vietcong and all those who have served with the Vietcong. Not infrequently Chiu-Hoi camps were raided by government troops, or the deserters were recruited into the Army, which was tantamount to breaking the promise that these people would not have to fight their one-time comrades in the Vietcong.

Some South Vietnamese governments have used the aid given them by the USA for the Chiu-Hoi programme for other purposes. Permission to build camps, permission to train the necessary rehabilitation personnel, even permission to pay the deserters often takes a long time to be granted. In spite of such obstacles, the Americans responsible for Chiu Hoi are pressing hard to make this project succeed. How little co-operation they get I realised when a South Vietnamese officer declared: 'Chiu Hoi? Oh, you mean the recreation areas for the Vietcong!'

It also happens that whole units of Vietcong, minus their weapons, give themselves up as deserters, spend six weeks being pampered in

Chiu Hoi and then return to their guerrilla units in the jungle complete with rice, seed, two suits and a large sum of money. None the less, since 1963 when the Americans began this project there have been 23,700 deserters of whom, according to JUSPAO, less than a thousand have defected back to the Vietcong.

6

HE was thirty-eight years old, a lieutenant-colonel in the South Vietnamese army, and for the past six months he had been the military governor of a province. As a sign of his rank he wore a red beret. He insisted on always going about unarmed, demonstrating that he was not afraid of the Vietcong, that he felt safe in his province and that the people were on his side.

The governor was waiting for me on the edge of an emergency airfield. Beyond I could see the members of his bodyguard, surrounding him about fifty yards away, their rifles, machine-pistols and machineguns at the ready. He was an energetic man, who had spent a year in America under training. He spoke fluent English. He had grasped, and this was obvious from all the conversations I had with him, exactly what had to be done in South Vietnam in order to win the 'hearts and minds' of the people.

'Only when the last Vietcong troops say they will no longer fight, that they want to stay in their village controlled and safeguarded by the government, when they lay down their arms and turn to the plough—only then will we have won the war,' he told me.

He invited me to breakfast and there I met three Americans. 'These are my advisers,' the military governor said. Two of them wore civilian clothes and one wore the uniform of a major. The first of these advisers was a professional civil servant, who was responsible for psychological warfare and was a member of JUSPAO. The second adviser specialised in social and economic questions. He was a member of USOM, which organises all the American material, as opposed to military, aid to Vietnam. The third adviser was in charge of the military operations in the province. He came under the supervision of MACV (Military Advisory Command Vietnam).

36

A few hours later I arrived at the headquarters of the regular American troops stationed in this province. The commanding officer welcomed me and introduced me to more 'advisers': a man from JUSPAO in charge of psychological warfare, and a man from USOM. But the difference was astounding. Whilst the American adviser was extremely reserved with the Vietnamese provincial governor and even addressed him as 'Sir' and 'With your permission, Sir', at the American headquarters it was the man from JUSPAO who called the tune.

And yet the duties of both JUSPAO advisers are very much alike. On the Vietnamese as on the American side they are in charge of psychological warfare. They don't sit around at headquarters. They are almost always on the move with the troops and with them in the front line—if there can be said to be any 'front lines' in Vietnam. There, at the front—or in the rear—they give advice to the South Vietnamese military governor and orders to the American military commander. Orders, that is, as to whether and how a village should be attacked.

'We never permit such an attack until the civilian population of the village has received thorough warning,' the political adviser explained. This is done by 'conventional' methods: helicopters with loudspeakers, leaflet raids and—wherever possible—by messengers sent into the villages. 'We call upon the civilians to leave the village. Sometimes they do as we say, very often not. In the beginning we relied on the fact that we had done our 'duty'. After due warning, the village was attacked. For the troops it was simply a Vietcong strongpoint, and they acted accordingly. When shots were fired from the houses, they fired back, using bazookas where necessary. I suppose you know all about this from reports in the world press.'

I knew. And I also knew what protests these reports had raised throughout the world. Usually the civilians had not left their villages, and often enough there were women and children in the houses and trenches under attack.

JUSPAO denies that it was the pressure of world public opinion which caused the USA to attach political advisers to all military commanders in Vietnam as well as to the South Vietnamese provincial governors. According to JUSPAO, they had intended to do this right from the start but due to the hurried build-up of so many

American troops and their rapid deployment at the front, political leadership lagged behind. Today the political experts are supposed to have the reins firmly in their hands. 'Nowadays there is hardly a military operation which has not previously been sanctioned by political advisers,' I was told.

'What happens now?' I asked.

'We have to accept that we must expose our troops to greater risks. They are not allowed to attack houses or even trenches if there is a danger that civilians may be harmed. It would be far easier if we could use tear-gas and other non-toxic gases, as we did at the start of our operations, then we could take the Vietcong alive. But we can no longer use these gases as a result of the pressure of world public opinion, so we have to risk the lives of our soldiers when we order them to go into the houses and trenches, spare the civilians and only shoot at the Vietcong.'

It is far easier to say this than to put it into practice, because the Vietcong now know that the Americans are handicapped by these orders, and thus they use women and children as shields. Wherever possible the American Department for Psychological Warfare still tries to put up loudspeakers, to get local civilians to speak to their fellow villagers and persuade the Vietcong to surrender. If it does come to a hand-to-hand fight for a village, however, these rules often have to go by the board. When it comes to shooting, it is every man for himself.

Civilian casualties are an inevitable daily occurrence in the Vietnamese war. What is the army's reaction to this policy of being kept under strict political control? 'This isn't a normal war. There's neither a front line nor a conventional enemy. To us this isn't a war at all. We are here to enforce a policy by means of military action,' a major explained to me. 'This was made abundantly clear to all our officers before we moved into Vietnam. All our troops know this and are reminded of it at least once a week. We are only here to carry out what is required of us by US policy. Political objectives have priority over every military operation.'

I pressed my point by asking whether this did not go against the grain. They admitted that it was often hard enough for the officers and especially for the men to discontinue an attack or deliberately to risk their own safety, but 'the President gave the order, these are our instructions and we have to keep to them'.

It is quite clear that the USA has placed its military forces in Vietnam under very extensive political control, not only at the top but right down to the smallest front-line unit.

'Out there in the field is where this psychological warfare begins,' I was told at JUSPAO headquarters in Saigon, 'but here it is our job to make this sort of warfare as successful as possible and as widespread as possible.' This entails:

Keeping the Vietnamese population constantly informed about the operations of US troops. This is done by using loudspeakers, leaflet raids, posters, newspapers, radio and by word of mouth.

Accounting for all US activities to the Vietnamese authorities and the Vietnamese army. This is done through liaison officers.

Continual advice to the Vietnamese Government and all Vietnamese authorities on questions of psychological warfare.

This last includes setting up printing presses, circulation of pamphlets, brochures, journals and newspapers; setting up complete radio stations, training announcers and commentators, advice on programme planning; training Vietnamese film and photography teams in making propaganda films and photographic exhibitions; setting up and equipping mobile cinemas and training the operators; advice and assistance in publishing newspapers, ranging from installing presses to supplying paper and technical staff.

In addition, the propaganda put out by all media in Vietnam has to be co-ordinated. Radio, cinema and the Press would be ineffective if those in charge did not know what message to give the people and how to put it across.

Along with the political advisory scheme for the American and South Vietnamese military commanders, an extensive briefing programme is also carried out for the troops. These troops are called upon to assist the population in all their needs. They are to take part in the transportation, rehousing (reconstruction of houses that have been destroyed), maintenance and even in entertainment. I frequently saw American soldiers building schools and kindergartens, helping to store rice in barns and lending a jeep to replace a buffalo for pulling a wagon or hauling a load. This is by no means entirely due to altruism.

'We're not angels,' they admitted at JUSPAO. 'These acts are the tools of psychological warfare which are going to help us to win the war.'

They openly admit that many of these methods, especially the direct aid to the population, were originally used by the Vietcong and they have had little hesitation in copying the enemy's methods, but since the Americans have considerably greater means at their disposal they hope to beat the Vietcong at their own game.

In the hinterland, however, a vast programme is being run by JUSPAO with the aim of awakening Vietnamese patriotism, national pride and, as far as possible, loyalty to the government. ('We have to tread very carefully. Here again we do nothing which the government has not requested or expressly sanctioned beforehand.') This programme includes the training of teachers, the rapid expansion of the school system, the production, printing and circulation of millions of textbooks, a comprehensive student exchange system, the recruiting of university professors from abroad to help in raising as rapidly as possible the Vietnamese academic level. Even the school syllabuses are being planned with American help.

I examined the syllabuses and the textbooks very carefully. There is not a single line advocating friendship with the USA or sympathy for the western way of life. On the contrary, they are aimed directly at Vietnamese national pride, encouraging belief in their own heritage, traditions and customs. Yet they are not reactionary: they accurately reflect the lot of the poor peasants and condemn grasping landowners. They call for social justice, respect for one's fellow citizens and equal rights for all, and they choose examples from Vietnamese history which are identical with the watchword of the French revolution: 'Liberty, equality, fraternity.'

This project has, of course, its special problems. The Vietnamese students who are recruited for it are politically conscious and they often oppose their own government, which they regard as undemocratic. As a result, the JUSPAO programme also includes what is known as 'motivation instruction'. This is instilled indirectly. The Americans instruct Vietnamese as 'agitators', who then explain to the people why there is still a war on in Vietnam, the aims of the war, why foreign troops are in Vietnam. The Vietnamese who have been instructed by this means then instruct more Vietnamese 'cadres' in their turn.

A word about this expression 'cadre'. It is used primarily by the communists. A 'cadre' is a man who knows the score and acts as a kind of on-the-spot information bureau and cheer-leader for government policy. I was astonished to hear in South Vietnam the word 'cadre' constantly used by Americans as well as by South Vietnamese government officials. Every official of JUSPAO or USOM, every government activist was called a 'cadre'. 'May I introduce our cadre Mr So-and-so,' I heard a dozen times a day.

These, in brief, are the most important functions of JUSPAO. They are also responsible for looking after all the press, radio and TV correspondents from all over the world (when I was in Saigon there were 324 of them), also an extensive programme for cultural development in Vietnam (libraries, adult literacy courses, English lessons, exhibitions, etc.), all in addition to JUSPAO's huge exertions to spread psychological warfare by all available media as far as North Vietnam.

At all events I now know, after several weeks of observing JUSPAO at work, why this mammoth enterprise is called a 'Joint' organisation. It requires a sustained co-operative effort to carry out all the points in their programme. The head of JUSPAO is one of the most capable men of the US Information Agency, Mr Zorthian—of Armenian descent. When JUSPAO started in Saigon the joke was 'What is JUSPAO? An Armenian word for chaos.' Since then, however, Mr Zorthian and his organisation have won a great deal of respect.

7

ON the edge of the jungle the battle was at its height. South Vietnamese troops were carrying out a mopping-up operation with the aim of driving Vietcong guerrillas out of the rice plantations and ensuring the safe harvesting of the crop.

A dark figure broke from the jungle opposite, ran across the ricefields pursued by several Vietnamese soldiers. He threw his tommy gun high in the air, raised his hands and sank to his knees. The man was, we discovered, a platoon leader of the Vietcong.

When interrogated he looked around him with eyes full of fear. They were very young eyes.

'How old are you?' asked the man conducting the trial.

The reply came hesitatingly, 'Eighteen.'

'I'll bet that fellow is no more than sixteen,' said the Vietnamese officer.

Sixteen years old, eighteen at the most, and already a Vietcong platoon leader. . . .

'They don't usually promote them so quickly—they haven't any more men left, that's all,' said the officer.

Whether that remark was wishful thinking or reality, I cannot say, but the fact remains that the boy before us was very young and had led a Vietcong platoon. That he, as leader of a unit, had been running in the wrong direction and, as he himself confessed, no longer knew where his own people or where the enemy were, made one think. The young man had obviously not received a very intensive or a very good military training. But what kind of political training had he had? The requirements expected of a Vietcong platoon leader—if the Vietcong are to continue to make headway—should, one supposes, be that he is both militarily and politically 'in the picture'. I could hardly believe that this captured NCO had been properly trained in either aspect.

The slogan about 'winning the hearts and minds' of the people is neither American nor South Vietnamese in origin, even though it is used by them. It was coined by Mao Tse-tung when he broke through the ring of troops besieging Kiang-si and began the 'Long March' with his troops. Mao Tse-tung expounded his strategy for winning the hearts and minds of the people in countless articles, and for years he put it into practice with his army. This is the strategy with which the Vietminh beat the French and with which the Vietcong are trying to conquer South Vietnam.

It is a simple but very effective strategy. A highly trained Vietcong cadre turns up in the village; he makes friends with the villagers and has nothing else to do but listen to their complaints. American counter-intelligence has an apt word for this activity—'consumer survey'. The cadre hears that the mayor is a power-seeker only interested in his own advancement; he hears that the people suffer heavily at the hands of the government tax collector; he hears of the landlord relentlessly collecting his exorbitant rents. There are also complaints that there are no schools in the village; that the sick have to die because they get no medical care; that no road has been built into the village to bring the rice to market; that the dams have been neglected and the irrigation system no longer works.

The women tell the communist cadre that they have no equal rights, that they are exploited by their menfolk who are backed up by tradition and outdated laws. The young people complain that their marriages are arranged by their parents and that they cannot marry whom they please. One man lacks money, another lacks a water buffalo.

The cadre takes back these consumer surveys to the headquarters of his Vietcong division. Shortly afterwards more cadres turn up at the same village. They speak the dialect of the villagers, as they are natives of that province. They know how to get on with the people. They know that it is not right to stand erect in front of them like a master facing his servants. They squat on the ground according to old Vietnamese custom and exchange courtesies. They talk about the weather, then they ask after the family and enquire about the sons and daughters.

Since these cadres have heard the 'consumer survey' of their colleagues, they are very well informed about the troubles and needs of nearly every single villager. They follow up this information. Yes, a schoolhouse could be built. One could even bring a teacher here. Even the building of a granary would be a simple matter. *You* need a water buffalo and *you* a little credit. A road—that could be built. Naturally, the village would need new wells. They talk to the women about emancipation and tell the young people that they may one day lead a better life in the towns.

There would of course be some conditions to comply with: the mayor would have to go, the government official would have to be done away with, the landowner would have to be expelled, a new village council would have to be formed. The villagers look anxious. How could they do all this without incurring the wrath of the government, without running the risk of a punitive expedition? But there is nothing simpler: they only have to take their fate into their own hands. The mayor, the government official, the landowner, they are only men— and they can die. Not murder. No, a trial by jury. A perfectly just trial. Haven't these people done a great deal of wrong? Yes, yes, a hundred times yes.

As for the government's punitive expedition, the answer is simple: self-protection. How? A Vietcong unit happens to be in the neighbourhood. They are good and brave men, say the cadres. They are on the side of justice. If they were approached they might be persuaded to take over the protection of the village.

Talks take place. It generally takes only a few days before the Vietcong move into the village. The mayor, the government official, the landowner (if he lives in the village) are immediately brought before a public tribunal. The verdict is quickly pronounced. The public pronounces it, incited by the Vietcong cadres. Very often it is death.

But it is not the Vietcong who give this verdict or carry it out. It is done by the population of the village, which incriminates them in the eyes of the government. This moment is of considerable psychological importance for the future activity of the Vietcong in the village, because from now on the whole community is afraid of government reprisals. From now on the Vietcong will be able to give orders which the villagers may not like, but which they must accept if they want to ensure Vietcong protection. Protection is now vital.

It would be wrong to imagine, however, that the Vietcong then take over, terrorising or looting. On the contrary. By means of the public trial and the collective death sentence passed on the ruling class of the village, they have acquired a means of blackmailing the community

44

—in case of need. Now the Vietcong try to put their promises into action. The landowner's property is divided, as is the plot which as common land belongs to the village, but which in most cases is illegally in the possession of the mayor. The common land is allotted to the peasants, at which the Vietcong take care *not* to remind them that according to the laws of the government the mayor never had been entitled to personal ownership of this land. It is referred to at this point as 'the mayor's land'. The Vietcong install a new mayor. It is this mayor who carries out the 'land reform' and sets the communal building scheme in motion. His small group of administrators are well trained and establish a reasonably effective village administration.

That is the so-called 'vertical' opening up of the village by the Vietcong. Simultaneously the 'horizontal' incision is made. Generally the Vietcong organise six village committees: (1) Farmers' Committee. (2) Workers' Committee. (3) Women's Committee. (4) Young People's Committee. (5) Students' Committee. (6) Committee for Cultural Activities.

Within the framework of these committees they try to comply with the wishes of the community. At the same time intensive ideological training is started. All inhabitants of the village belong to one or other of the six committees and are often summoned to evening meetings. Political training is therefore carried on outside the jurisdiction of the village council, which concerns itself only with 'administrative' matters. Requests which concern the interests of the various groups are passed on from the committees to the village council.

The ingenuity of this procedure lies in the fact that the village councils very often lack the material resources to grant the requests. The Party (which is not called the Communist Party in South Vietnam, but the National Liberation Front, although it is communist-run and carries out communist orders) thereby ensures that any recriminations are aimed not against itself, but against the new mayor, who can be removed from office if necessary without any political harm either to the party or to the Vietcong. Consequently the mayor nominated by the Vietcong is in most cases neither a member of the Vietcong nor of the Party. He is just a tool of the Vietcong.

Once Vietcong influence has been firmly established in the village, then the other side of the picture begins to emerge. It is made clear to the community that they are not going to enjoy all this progress for

45

nothing. Now they have to fulfil their part of the bargain. To support the administration, the full-time party cadres and above all the troops (who of course protect the village from the government) tax has to be paid: 20 to 30 per cent of the rice harvest. This tax is roughly equivalent to that demanded by the government, though it is lower than the rent previously payable to the landowner.

The youth of the village also has to make sacrifices—boys and girls of military age are recruited into Vietcong service. Two promises are then given to them: they will fight in the neighbourhood of their own village, or at least in their home territory, and will not be sent further afield. Should they be killed in action their bodies will be brought home in accordance with the deeply rooted Vietnamese reverence for their departed ancestors.

The young people who have been incorporated into the Committee for Students, however, although they have perhaps never even attended primary school, have been selected by the cadres for their high intelligence and have been promised the chance to study. They receive special training and are recruited as potential party members. Middle-aged men and women are organised into work battalions and porterage squads. They have to work on village building projects and they have to maintain supplies to the fighting troops in the jungle.

It would be wrong to suppose that these measures by themselves make the Vietcong unpopular. The cadres are very skilful in explaining the need for these sacrifices, which are generally recognised by the community. They are even grateful that 'so much' is being done for them, because in comparison with what they had before, it is a lot. Furthermore over the past few years the population has been firmly convinced that the Vietcong were unbeatable, that they were the government of tomorrow and that everyone was well advised to be on good terms with their future rulers.

To return to the captured Vietcong platoon leader. An eighteen-year-old with obviously very limited military and political training, he was hardly capable of carrying out such an exacting programme. I found it difficult to believe that he was of the stuff with which the Vietcong could hope to win the 'hearts and minds' of the population.

'They have lost too many cadres and they have no more well-trained men to replace them with,' said the South Vietnamese officer.

However, two questions still remained: why were the Vietcong unable to win the South Vietnamese population to their side in past years when they still had enough good cadres? And what is the consequence for the Vietcong today of their heavy loss of cadres?

When one studies the Vietcong's system of winning over a village, one is forced to admit the effectiveness of their methods, yet ultimate success has so far been denied the Vietcong in Vietnam—and not only for military reasons.

8

IT happened in one of the sprawling suburbs of Saigon. The taxi-driver had deposited me, as Saigon taxi-drivers often do, in the wrong place and at the other end of the town. So I wandered about the narrow streets, trying to make myself understood, but everyone I spoke to apparently knew nothing but Vietnamese. Then, to cap it all, a tropical storm broke and in a matter of minutes the water in the streets was ankle-deep.

According to everything I had been told about safety in Saigon, I was supposed to avoid taking shelter in any of the low Vietnamese houses. As I stood there undecidedly, I suddenly got the feeling that every passerby was a Vietcong. And all the time there was non-stop thunder and lightning. I confess that I was far from happy. It must have shown, for all of a sudden two or three Vietnamese stood in front of me, grinning broadly, and offering me their raincoats. Others invited me to shelter in their shops or homes. In no time I felt safe again and knew that I wasn't among enemies—and they did not know that I was not an American.

This little episode, and so much of my previous and subsequent experience, showed me that there was apparently no hatred or even dislike of the white foreigner. It could therefore hardly be true that the sympathies of the population were really with the Vietcong. 'You will find this in other places besides Saigon,' a European correspondent told me an hour later. He had already spent several years stationed in Vietnam. 'The Vietcong have lost a lot of sympathisers and in the territories which they control they govern more by fear and pressure than by popularity.'

How could this be explained? Since the partition of the country in

1954 the South Vietnamese regimes have been anything but popular governments, whilst the Vietcong have made every effort to win the sympathies of the people. I tried to analyse this phenomenon during many discussions with politicians, students, Buddhists, peasants and people on all levels of society. The answers I received were often startling.

The Vietcong's great misfortune lies in the fact that communism has already been in power for more than ten years in North Vietnam. When the communists gained power in Hanoi in 1954 they started to build up a people's democracy mainly on Chinese lines. As with all people's democracies founded under the guidance of Stalin or Mao Tse-tung, the state consolidated its power by means of far-reaching purges, terror and concentration camps. In addition, the North Vietnamese are a very militant people, the opposite of the Russians and the Chinese. For Vietnam is by no means populated by one race alone, but by the Tonkinese in the North, the Annamites in Central Vietnam and the Cochin-Chinese in the South. The differences in language as well as national character are profound. To take a European parallel, the Tonkinese in the North resemble the Spartans and the Cochin-Chinese in the South are Athenians, or—according to a contemporary comparison current in Saigon—the Tonkinese are the 'Prussians' and the South Vietnamese the 'Bavarians' of Vietnam.

'When you judge Vietnam, always bear this comparison in mind and then you will be able to understand this country and its people far better,' I was told in Saigon.

Since they themselves had very little political experience, the North Vietnamese communists stuck to the Stalinist pattern of class war and with their own characteristic thoroughness carried this class warfare to such extremes that they apparently put Stalin and Mao Tse-tung in the shade. They aimed not only at exterminating the 'enemy of the people' but—following Stalin's example—also at unmasking and destroying the enemies in their own party. There are said to have been blood-baths in North Vietnam incomparably more savage than even the measures taken under Stalin.

Their slogan is said to have been that even the most faithful party member was not to be trusted but was liable to be hauled before a 'people's' tribunal. At first the party cadres played their part. They forced better-off peasants and 'bourgeois' to make public confessions at mock trials, condemned them to death and had them hanged, but when pressure from above increased and the party cadres were ordered to find still more 'enemies of the people', when the cadres realised that any further executions would affect party members and when they saw that this mass slaughter was defeating the fundamental aims of the Party, they frequently refused to go on with the purge.

Then it was the turn of the party cadres themselves, who were hunted down whenever someone accused them. To this day there is still no logical explanation for this twist of policy, which undoubtedly originated from the top. Undeniably, many hundreds of party cadres were murdered after the purge. The North Vietnamese government never revealed the number of dead. But the present North Vietnamese Defence Minister, General Giap, announced after the 20th Party Congress of the Communist Party of the Soviet Union (Khrushchev's 'de-stalinisation' congress) that as many as 12,000 party members and officials had been released from prison, meaning those who had been arrested as a result of the purge. Those who had been executed could no longer be released. As in the Soviet Union, however, many of them were posthumously rehabilitated.

The leading North Vietnamese paper, *Nhan Dan*, published a verbatim account of General Giap's speech at the 10th Congress of the Central Committee on October 31, 1956. According to this not only the rich but also the 'middling' peasants were killed during the blood-bath. No consideration was given to families whose sons were serving in the Vietminh or with the army; soldiers and officers who had served gallantly with the Liberation Army (against the French) were tortured, imprisoned or executed; the chiefs of the numerous North Vietnamese mountain tribes were killed, the people routed and scattered, and finally, explained General Giap, the terror was turned against party members and during this period 'torture was common practice'. I am purposely quoting only North Vietnamese communist sources. When one reads South Vietnamese statistics on the persecutions or the reports of international commissions of enquiry, a far blacker picture emerges.

All this, of course, happened before 1956, before Stalinism had been denounced within the world communist movement. In the Soviet Union and in the Eastern European people's democracies, the post-1956 governments compensated for some of the harm done by adopting a more liberal attitude—or at least by proclaiming a change of heart. Similar moves took place in North Vietnam. There too liberalisation and moderation were the order of the day. But the people did not forget the trauma so quickly and—more significantly—a large section of the South Vietnamese population had heard what had taken place in the North. There were far too many family ties, far too many refugees from the North and the South Vietnamese government made sure that the Communist purges were given wide currency in the South. Even the finest-sounding Vietcong social programmes and land reforms were scarcely much help.

Nor are conditions in Vietnam comparable to those in China, where the peasants had once led an unbearable existence persecuted by local warlords and grasping landowners. In Vietnam there has always been common land in every village. Vietnamese landowners as such never became such a social menace as in China because the French colonial rulers converted a good part of the arable land into plantations. Hatred of these plantation owners was a hatred of foreigners, but was not directed against local exploiters.

Furthermore there was the comparatively good road and rail network (built by the French) in Vietnam which provided good communications between town and country, between provinces and between families. For years radio sets were widespread in Vietnamese villages. A multitude of newspapers were read too, so that whatever happened in North Vietnam was soon known in the South.

The Vietcong worked strenuously to impress on the southerners that there had been 'mistakes' in the North, that things were going to be done far better in the South and that after the seizure of power by the National Liberation Front the South Vietnamese would not suffer the same fate as their brothers in the North. In view of this severe handicap, it is in fact astonishing how much support the Vietcong was still able to gain. To do so they relied on a number of factors.

First and foremost they required a well-trained body of cadres—leaders who had not only had a complete military training but who were also skilled political tacticians. The combination of these two qualities resulted—as we now know—in irreparable losses to the Vietcong. The good military leader tends to figure prominently in military operations. He charges ahead of his troops and as a result the good cadres head the casualty lists. Over the past three years the Vietcong are said to have lost at least 6,000 such cadre officers in this way alone. This figure is based on the number of cadre officers whose bodies have been picked up by government troops. How many were killed whose bodies have not been recovered remains a matter of speculation.

The cadres—military as well as political—are difficult to replace, especially in a country in which the Vietcong are on a permanent war footing. It is even harder today now that non-stop American air attack makes training in safe provinces almost an impossibility. In consequence the Vietcong have had to resort to importing cadre officers from the North. It is not always successful when North Vietnamese, i.e. Tonkinese and Annamites, are put in command of South Vietnamese Vietcong units. The South Vietnam 'Athenians' are made to obey the 'Spartans' from North Vietnam.

This has probably improved the Vietcong regular army's military standing, but the bulk of the Vietcong consists of irregulars, peasant youths who are briefly trained and then serve as guerrillas in the Vietcong ranks. They no longer understand the language of their superiors. Or rather they do—and they hate it, because the differences between North, Central and Southern Vietnam are enormous.

It is even more difficult when cadres from the North have to carry out political work in South Vietnamese villages. They have to deal with very stubborn and often narrow-minded peasants. The crucial point in the Vietcong's political work, however, has always been their campaign to win people's confidence. They are understandably no longer very successful at this. They know it themselves, and they are forced to recruit the lower ranks of the Vietcong from young South Vietnamese. The latter are, however, uneducated and it must often be hard for the Vietcong to decide whether to leave the leadership of a village in the hands of good, but unpopular, officers from the North or of militarily and politically poorly trained junior officers from the South.

As a result the war in South Vietnam has changed in character: the cadre officers from the North have far less consideration for the needs of the people in the South. Their families do not live here. They are strangers on foreign soil. They obey orders from the North without, as they say in communist jargon, always taking the 'concrete conditions and local requirements' in the South into consideration. The population notices this and the word goes round. In recent months the

Vietcong have been deprived of bases by non-stop American bombing and surprise attacks. They are never left in peace. Worried, harassed, badly provisioned Vietcong cadres can no longer take 'political' action when they need rice, money and new recruits. Force has now replaced the Vietcong's original kid-glove treatment of the population.

This has resulted in the rapid rise of refugees from Vietcong areas and a drastic increase in the number of deserters from Vietcong ranks, who bring the government and the Americans something which hitherto they have seriously lacked: information on the Vietcong and their movements. This in turn increases the success of government troops and American military operations, and forces the Vietcong to take even more desperate measures. Yet Saigon by no means regards the Vietcong as defeated. They respect the courage, toughness and determination of its cadres. They know that these people often achieve the impossible and the repeated surprise successes of the Vietcong prove this.

'But,' I was told, 'we also know, and most of the population know it too, that the promises of the Vietcong, their land reform, their declarations of equal rights for all citizens are no longer credible. The people suspect that all these promises are only moves to help win the guerrilla war and set up a communist dictatorship. What will follow afterwards is evident from reports from North Vietnam. This is why there is still a general dislike of the Vietcong prevalent in South Vietnam—amounting in many cases to hatred—in spite of the repeated failures of the South Vietnamese governments. The South Vietnamese may sometimes not know what they are fighting for, but they know pretty clearly what they are fighting against.'

This is how the Americans assess the situation. They are, however, under no illusions. At the moment it is the tremendous pressure exerted by American troops which has forced the Vietcong to limit their political agitation and virtually to abandon their partially successful socio-economic programme. If the Vietcong were given a breathing space they could reinforce their cadres and if they had the time and opportunity for active political warfare they would remain a dangerous and effective adversary.

'We must therefore carry out a constructive economic programme alongside our military operations,' say South Vietnamese and Americans alike. 'The aim of this plan must be to reorganise the whole economic and social structure of South Vietnam and in effect to transform it completely. We have to show results which outstrip the promises made by the Vietcong. Above all, the difference between a free social system and a communist dictatorship must be clearly illustrated in the way we treat the people.'

In order to accomplish this the Americans have backed up the South Vietnamese government with an organisation which has already been mentioned several times previously—USOM. Next to the army, this is the most important instrument in deciding the result of the war in Vietnam.

9

'GENTLEMEN, I must apologise on the doctor's behalf. He won't be joining us until after supper.' My host was a twenty-eight-year-old American and I was in a South Vietnamese province about 200 miles north-east of Saigon. The American was in charge of the local outpost of USOM, through which all the non-military American aid to Vietnam is channelled. The doctor whose absence he had just excused was one of his most important colleagues. For this Vietnamese doctor is the only one in the province and theoretically he has no less than 28,000 patients to look after.

The doctor was late that evening because several ambulances had arrived at his hospital during the afternoon. The patients they brought were not wounded, nor were they soldiers. They were civilians, peasants from the surrounding villages, and they had a disease which centuries ago was very well known in Europe—the plague. There was an outbreak of plague in the province.

'Towards the end of the monsoon season the plague always breaks out here,' explained the USOM official. 'Last year we had a bad time of it. The new hospital was not yet ready, it was difficult to isolate the patients and we didn't have enough drugs. This year things are much better.'

Nowadays the plague is no longer such a dangerous disease. If diagnosed reasonably early and treated with modern antibiotics every patient can be saved, provided that these conditions are fulfilled. Until recently this often didn't happen. There were not and still are not enough doctors. In South Vietnam there are only 280 doctors available for a population of 14 million, for until recently there was no medical faculty in this country, and only those who could afford to study abroad became doctors.

The doctor arrived very late that evening—worn out from his work and suffering from exhaustion. He invited me to visit the hospital on the next day. 'It will interest you. You can learn a lot from seeing it.'

The hospital was built by USOM. It is a modern, spacious provincial hospital. It is supplied with the best technical equipment which has all been brought over from the USA. But there was a small kerosene lamp next to each bed and the operating theatre had never been in use.

'Come with me. I'll show you something.' The doctor took my arm and led me down to the cellar. Here was a large generator—thirteen feet high. 'General Electric' I read. Underneath I saw the emblem of the handshake and the star-spangled banner—the sign for American aid. 'This generator was delivered to us by USOM almost a year ago.' But it is not connected up. It doesn't work. USOM built the hospital, provided all the equipment, but the electricity cables should have been laid by the South Vietnamese. 'For the past year we have been trying in vain to get an electrician to come from Saigon,' said the doctor despondently. The USOM official looked no happier either, but he at least was hopeful. There are electricians among the American army troops who have come to Vietnam.

The remainder of the day was spent in a small column of jeeps, under the protection of a half-platoon of South Vietnamese paratroops, visiting the surrounding villages. Wherever we went the people gave us a lively, friendly welcome. 'No Vietcong?' I asked. 'Oh, yes,' replied the USOM official. 'The Vietcong come during the night. And now that the rice crops are being harvested, they'll be coming in the daytime, too.'

There was hardly any doubt here on which side the sympathy of the people lay. Nor was there any question why they showed such sympathy. In this district, with the help of a team of their own Americans and Filipinos, USOM had constructed dozens of new wells, large storehouses and granaries, many schools and medical stations, several experimental farms for improving the rice output, cattle-rearing stations and accommodation for thousands of refugees. Moreover, they had brought all the necessary teaching staff into the province. They had come from teacher-training institutes which have also been built, equipped and financed by USOM.

USOM flew many hundreds of tons of rice into the province when in the previous year the Vietcong took almost half the rice harvest away from the farmers. They also helped out with edible oil and kerosene. They constructed bridges, dams and irrigation systems. And they gave the fishermen on the coast of the province outboard motors for their hitherto slow-moving fishing boats. In contrast to the generator at the hospital, these other projects initiated by USOM had worked.

Who serves in USOM? Only two of the USOM officials were married. Their wives were with them and taught English in Vietnamese schools. All USOM officials are civilians. Originally they were not in the service of the American government but belonged to an institution on which the present American Peace Corps was apparently based. It is called International Field Service—an organisation founded by the combined churches in America. The majority of USOM officials whom I met in Vietnam had already been here for two to four years. Their ranks have been thinned by the Vietcong, yet they refuse to carry pistols. Many of them already speak fluent Vietnamese and not infrequently live with Vietnamese families.

'Our most difficult problem is land reform,' explained the USOM man. 'Whatever they may say in Saigon—they maintain that land reform in Vietnam is not so important because most of the farmers already have land—out here the need for land is great. And the Vietcong promise to satisfy it.' Land reform is firmly written into the South Vietnamese constitution and has been for the last ten years. 'But until now little has been done.'

The government bought the land from the French plantation owners at a considerable price. These large plantation areas were allocated for land reform. The government had, moreover, directed that the common land of each village should be divided among the villagers. This amounts to roughly 20 per cent of the cultivated land. And they forced the landowners to sell all land over 250 acres to the government, who parcelled it out among the farmers. Even so, 250 acres can still be a sharp thorn in the side of those who cultivate it as tenants, especially when the landowner collects a ground rent of 50 per cent and sometimes even 70 per cent of the harvest, and not 25 per cent as stipulated.

USOM officials look on and can only grind their teeth. They don't admit it, but one can feel that they see all their work threatened by this. In South Vietnam, however, nothing can be done if it is not the government's wish and USOM are therefore trying hard to counteract the negative results of the only partially successful land reform; bulldozers and tractors are used by USOM to clear the jungle, dig wells and construct irrigation systems in order to obtain additional land for distribution under the terms of the land reform. This is often tragic to watch. On the one hand enormous areas of fertile land which have not been divided up because they belong to an influential man, and on the other USOM teams wresting new land out of the jungle, simply in order to make the land reform effective. They often have to look on with their hands tied while the old system of rack-renting landlords continues to flourish.

USOM also has other responsibilities. 'The most important part of our programme lies in getting the population to co-operate,' assert USOM officials. 'We bring the material, we draw up the plans, we provide the machinery. But we call upon the people themselves to pitch in and help on all projects.'

This has not always been so. At the beginning of the USOM programme a lot of building was done in which the people took no part, or which was paid for. When the Vietcong then destroyed the American projects, the people hardly felt this as a loss. Now that they regard each of these projects as their own, they are generally left untouched by the Vietcong. For the villagers are proud of their school, their storehouse and their paved streets.

USOM men have every reason to be satisfied with their work. They could, however, do much more if they had their own funds. The finances for all their projects are in fact provided by the USA but they are handed over to the Vietnamese government. Each USOM project has consequently to be sanctioned by this government, and it is the government who then allocates the American money—changed into Vietnamese piastres. 'And that can take months. Sometimes even more than a year,' USOM cadres complain, 'especially when the government is in a crisis, when new ministers and new officials are responsible for expenditure.' But here too the Americans respect the sovereignty of the Vietnamese and financial aid continues to be administered by the government.

There are other setbacks. The supplies of rice, edible oil and other consumer goods provided by USOM are handed over to the Vietnamese provincial authorities for distribution. In some provinces with energetic young provincial governors this distribution works perfectly. In others, part of the aid disappears in the pipeline. Even when distribution works, considerable harm is often done. How does one distribute goods which cost nothing? They are meant for those in need, so they are given to religious institutions. This can go wrong, for these institutions don't need the rice; what they need is money. So they sell the rice. Doubtless in order to raise funds for charity. But those who buy the rice and see the American Aid sign on the sacks can hardly be expected to believe afterwards that this American Aid was free. Similar difficulties occur with rice allocations which are given to South Vietnamese soldiers for special bravery or for the capture of Vietcong weapons. They too often turn their premium into cash and demand high black market prices into the bargain.

Notwithstanding these setbacks, USOM is a policy instrument of the Vietnamese government and of the USA, to be used for conquering the Vietcong in what is by far the most important campaign on the social and economic front.

'How much time can you spare?' I was asked at the enormous complex of buildings which houses USOM headquarters in Saigon. It takes several hours to cover all the activities of USOM. Here in summary are just the most important USOM projects in Vietnam:

Standard Aid. This includes the construction of primary schools, secondary schools, teacher-training institutes, university institutes, the training of lecturers and professors, construction of health centres and hospitals, roads, bridges, railways, airfields, irrigation projects, dams, wells, storehouses and granaries, construction of covered markets, distribution of artificial fertilisers, building power stations and reservoirs; the installation of a nationwide telephone network; the recruitment of doctors and technical instructors; the compiling, printing and distribution of millions of school textbooks; the setting up of a strong fishing fleet; the fight against epidemics; the supply of drugs; and—USOM's special pride—the establishment of a college for public

59

administration to give Vietnam a modern, efficient administrative system.

The most costly item in the USOM programme is supporting the state budget. In 1964 alone the USA channelled 200 million dollars via USOM into Vietnam's normal budget in order to support the piastre and to maintain price stability in the country. 'Because this is the third front on which we could lose the war—the price front.' This support also covers the importation of rice, petrol, diesel oil, iron and steel products, machinery and all kinds of consumer goods to the value of 190 million dollars for the year 1964 only. The Americans are repaid not more than 10 per cent of this sum in piastres—to provide wages for the local labour employed by them.

USOM is also responsible for establishing and equipping a strong civilian police organisation. Police barracks, police stations, mobile police units and equipping the police with the most up-to-date weapons are USOM concerns. 'For the Vietcong is to a large extent a police problem. The more this police force can track down weapons and bombs, the more accurately informed they can be on local conditions in the villages and towns, the harder it will be for the Vietcong to infiltrate and sabotage.'

The most extensive USOM project, however, is that of agricultural reconstruction. I have already described in part how this is carried out. It includes tilling new land, building roads to market towns, wells, dams and irrigation works, storehouses and granaries, village schools and health centres, providing further education and payment to teachers and doctors, training hospital nurses and midwives, distributing artificial fertilisers, teaching new farming methods, improving cattle breeding, giving direct aid to farmers and much else beside.

They say at USOM: 'We are working on the basis that this is a politico-economic and social war which at the moment only has military overtones. Further, that it is a Vietnamese and by no means an American war. And that this war can only be won by revolution. A revolution which will involve the mass of the Vietnamese population, the vast majority of whom are peasants.'

Thus USOM pays, via the government, for all the material requirements for land reform and can only hope that the government will soon decide on more drastic reform measures.

Finally, USOM is largely responsible for looking after the one million refugees from North Vietnam and the 800,000 refugees from the Vietcong territories in South Vietnam: for their accommodation, food, rehousing, retraining, clothing and every other need.

But even USOM cannot work miracles. It will take years before their work shows adequate results. I have personally seen the difficulties they have to face and what setbacks they have to reckon with. These setbacks can generally be traced to the administrative failures of the South Vietnamese government. The government is, however, the key to the present and, above all, to the future of South Vietnam. The Americans can step in with military power, they can give economic aid, but they will never be able to bring ultimate peace or even social stability to Vietnam. Only a good Vietnamese government can do this, but the developments in the South Vietnamese government have never been very encouraging.

IO

THE mayor of the South Vietnamese town of Da Nang pointed to a piece of land lying on the opposite river bank. Two years ago it had been decided to build a large housing estate over there, an estate badly needed to house the many refugees in the town. Two years ago that land was handed over to the municipal authorities by the government for this purpose, then the money for the project was sanctioned. But to this day the mayor has not received the money.

The money came from American Aid funds. The South Vietnamese prime minister, Kanh, approved the building of the houses and made the money available, but before Saigon had transferred the funds the Kanh government toppled.

The mayor of Da Nang applied to the new government. Some weeks later a commission arrived, inspected the land, assessed the importance of the project, came to the same conclusion as the first commission, recommended the financing of the project and the new government acquiesced. But before the authorities had time to pay the money over, this government also fell. A new commission arrived, examined the project—and so the story goes on, over and over again.

Recently the present prime minister of Vietnam, Air Vice-Marshal Ky, came to Da Nang, had everything explained to him by the mayor and promised to get the money transferred immediately. By the time that I came to Vietnam, the mayor of Da Nang had not yet been able to lay the first brick in this venture which has had top priority for years.

The problem of the mayor of Da Nang illuminates one aspect of the struggle in Vietnam which until now has proved the biggest obstacle to the government's success: the discord at the top, the inability to put a popular government at the helm which could give the country firm, clear-sighted leadership whilst being as democratic as possible.

The causes of this political weakness originated when Vietnam was part of French Indo-China. But they also stem from the period when the democratic revolutionary, Dr Sun Yat-sen, was leading his 'National People's Party'—the Kuomintang—in the Chinese town of Canton and attempting to conquer China. That was at the beginning of the 1920s.

Sun Yat-sen had made a pact between Kuomintang and China's Communist Party. His military academy was at that time under the leadership of General Chiang Kai-shek, whose second-in-command was Chou En-lai. In his 'political bureau' there sat a man whose name was Mao Tse-tung. And one of the junior instructors in the military academy of the Kuomintang was called Nguyen Ai Quoc, known throughout the world today as Ho Chi Minh. He is now the President of communist North Vietnam. He was thus a contemporary of Chiang Kai-shek, of Mao Tse-tung and of Chou En-lai who formed the Kuomintang-Communist coalition.

Like them, Ho Chi Minh also believed in democracy in his very early days, then in social democracy, till he finally landed in the communist camp. He too, as so many of todays' communist leaders in China, had travelled all over the world. He had been a ship's cook, a labourer, a student. He visited the USA, England, France, Germany, Russia. He collaborated on social democratic newspapers in Europe and he believed in the liberation of his country from colonial rule by national insurrection, by a democratic Vietnamese people's movement.

The end of the First World War and the installation of colonial rule under the terms of the Treaty of Versailles disappointed him as it did the many Chinese politicians. When the Second International, in which social democrats and communists still sat together, came to a stormy end, Ho Chi Minh, as one of the delegates, advocated the setting up of the Third International and thus acknowledged himself for the first time as a communist sympathiser.

As a communist official, Ho Chi Minh was posted to Sun Yat-sen's headquarters in Canton. As a communist agent he founded the Vietnamese Youth Movement there. Many of those young Vietnamese who fled from French Indo-China and sought contact with the very influential Sun Yat-sen were recruited by the then Nguyen Ai Quoc—Ho Chi Minh—for his youth movement. He also gave them a communist political training. Not all of his students agreed with his teaching. Many of them did not want to have anything to do with communism and supported Sun Yat-sen's Kuomintang—in fact, they later founded a 'National People's Party' for Vietnam which was to be the spearhead of the revolt against the French.

It is today an acknowledged fact that Ho Chi Minh was already paving the way for the ultimate triumph of his party, while his Youth Movement was putting these nationalist Vietnamese on black lists.

They allegedly had a threefold value for the Vietnamese Communist Party: when members of this nationalist group returned to Vietnam, the French consul in Hongkong received their names, photographs and the approximate date of their arrival in Vietnam. It was easy for the French security police in Vietnam to arrest them. Ho Chi Minh's communist Youth Movement supposedly received generous sums of money as premiums per head from the French authorities. In this way the communists filled their empty coffers—or so it is said.

When at one stage Ho Chi Minh was accused of being an informer for the French, he denied that he had actually collaborated (as he denied, for a long time, being Nguyen Ai Quoc) but was supposed to have admitted that this sort of deal had occurred and that these activities had been of great importance for the nationalist movement in Vietnam.

For that was the second advantage of the extradition of the Vietnamese national revolutionaries: their arrest by the French became known, thus stirring up hatred against colonial rule and spreading a spirit of revolution through Vietnam, particularly when the more prominent among these nationalist revolutionaries were tried and executed by the French.

The third advantage was to be apparent much later: in 1944, when the first organised hostilities in Vietnam took place against the French, in the late 1940s when the Vietnamese united front against colonial power was formed and the so-called Vietminh instigated the ultimate battle for the freedom of Vietnam, the nationalist camp in Vietnam had only a few leaders to offer. The communists, however, were practically at full strength. So it was comparatively easy for the communists to dominate the Vietminh, to set themselves at the head of the struggle for liberation and to override the weakened rump of the Vietnamese Kuomintang.

In surveying Ho Chi Minh's life and work between 1925 and 1941, it is significant that when the red-blue coalition in China broke down and Chiang Kai-shek took up his fight against the communists, Ho Chi Minh together with the staff of the Soviet Consulate in Canton fled first to Shanghai and then to Moscow. As early as then he had a Soviet passport, which he had been given as an 'interpreter' for the Soviet Consulate.

It was in 1941, following Germany's attack on the Soviet Union that Ho was ordered by Stalin to go to Mao Tse-tung in North China and from there to investigate the possibility of a communist advance into Indo-China. Ho did not wait for Mao Tse-tung's victory in China. He set out on his journey to Indo-China with false papers and under different names, and he reached Vietnam in 1942 when the Japanese allowed the French, in accordance with the Vichy settlement, to continue ruling Indo-China.

After the attack on Pearl Harbor in 1941, the Japanese marched through Indo-China during their advance on Singapore and Indonesia, but in order to avoid the problems of an army of occupation and a complicated administrative system, they allowed French colonial rule to function undisturbed until the end of the war.

'The communists couldn't have had better conditions,' I was told by a Saigon university professor, who had himself worked with the underground at that time. 'We in Vietnam had hoped that Japan, an Asiatic power, would free us from colonial rule. But Japan not only attacked neighbouring China, which was a great blow to us, she then went on to support colonial rule in Vietnam. From then on there was in fact only one party which advocated fighting for freedom against all our enemies—the communists. They urged war against Japan and could point to the example of Mao Tse-tung, who had also fought the Japanese in China. And they called for insurrection against the French.'

A further consequence was the founding, at this period, of the 'League for Vietnamese Independence' by Ho Chi Minh and his Communist Party—an institution which from now on was to be known to the world as the Vietminh. Ho Chi Minh knew exactly how to gain support for the Vietminh from all nationalist revolutionary groups. 'For all of us the Vietminh was the only hope,' added the professor.

The Vietminh formed the first guerrilla units in Indo-China, and then operated primarily against the Japanese, which was reason enough for the Americans and British to side with this resistance movement. Soon American and British planes were making night flights to Vietnam dropping weapons and radio transmitters to the Vietminh guerrillas, as they dropped weapons and transmitters in Europe to Tito in Yugoslavia. The Vietminh under the leadership of Ho Chi Minh delivered the goods. Not only were Japanese units rounded up and destroyed, but innumerable American and British airmen who were forced down in this area were looked after by Vietminh troops, cared for, fed and taken through Burma back to the British lines. Today the Americans still sometimes find a light automatic pistol of American manufacture dating back to 1943 lying beside the body of a Vietcong casualty.

The final days of the war in Vietnam were very turbulent. The French officers, bound by oath in 1941 to the pro-German government in Vichy, were far from home at the time of the liberation of France by the American and British troops and the forces of General de Gaulle. It was obvious to them that they had to act quickly if they were to be called good patriots after the war, so they decided to rebel against the Japanese.

It was on March 9, 1945, that the French in Vietnam planned to open their attack. The Japanese found out, quelled the revolt, disarmed the French soldiers and imprisoned the officers. Interestingly enough, the Japanese allowed the French-sponsored Emperor of Vietnam, Bao Dai, to remain on the throne, but they forced him to form a pro-Japanese government—another factor which favoured the Vietminh. For this government under Bao Dai was in fact pro-Japanese yet still sufficiently nationalistic—being anti-French—to release all the Vietminh leaders who had been arrested by the French, including a good number of communists.

The Vietminh prepared for the final battle. 'I well remember August 19, 1945,' continued the professor. 'The Japanese capitulated. The French were scarcely in evidence any more, since they were still held in Japanese custody. It took one day for the Vietnamese units to occupy Hanoi, the capital of North Vietnam. Ho Chi Minh was declared President of the provisional government of the Democratic Republic of Vietnam. We national revolutionaries were alarmed, but the real power lay with Ho Chi Minh. Furthermore, Ho was the only real leader left in our ranks. He had dedicated his life to the fight for freedom in Vietnam. His authority was undisputed.'

When one talks to the American experts on Vietnamese policy today, they say: 'In those days it might still perhaps have been possible to make a national leader out of Ho Chi Minh—a Tito. He was a man whose Vietnamese national consciousness had also rebelled against China. The Vietnamese and Chinese were fundamentally hostile to each other. Vietnam had been under Chinese rule for 1,300 out of 2,000 years. But we missed our opportunity of winning Ho Chi Minh over.'

In fact, in 1945, Ho Chi Minh was only able to enjoy his new status as president of a free Vietnam for a very short period. While his guerrilla units were taking Hanoi, the British were landing in Saigon. And the Allies implored their Chinese colleague, Chiang Kai-shek, to march into Indo-China in order to disarm the Japanese there and guarantee the safety of the country.

Ho Chi Minh, astonished and in despair at this turn of events, found, as so often in his career, unexpected help. The nationalist revolutionaries in Vietnam, many of them members of the Vietnamese Kuomintang, regarded the advancing Chinese as genuine allies. Thus with the help of the Nationalist Chinese they tried to drive out the communists. But in Paris General de Gaulle was preparing for the reconquest of Indo-China. He reached an agreement with Chiang Kai-shek that the Chinese troops would withdraw from Vietnam as soon as the newly armed French expeditionary force reached Indo-China, which duly took place.

When the Kuomintang troops left Vietnam, Ho Chi Minh attacked those nationalist revolutionaries who had allied themselves with the Chinese. When he was reproached that he would thus be siding with the French, Ho Chi Minh is supposed to have said: 'It would be better to be stuck under the French yoke for ten years than to rot for another thousand years in the Chinese mire.'

And so Ho Chi Minh again became a temporary ally of the French. In March 1946 an agreement was reached between the Vietminh and France by which the Vietnamese Republic would become part of the 'French Union' as a free state with its own government, its own parliament, its own army and its own financial system, leaving France as just the protector of Vietnam.

The French, however, only adhered to this agreement until their troops had occupied the whole of Vietnam. On December 19, 1946, the Vietminh troops raided a newly built French barracks. This was the beginning of a communist war of independence against France which lasted for nearly nine years. It was to have its climax and ultimate victory in the siege of Dien Bien Phu.

II

MAY 7, 1954, went down in history as one of the blackest days in the annals of the French army. On that day the exhausted remnants of a French parachute battalion hoisted the white flag in a little village in Vietnam which was scarred and furrowed by bombs and shells. The name of the village was Dien Bien Phu. Yet the troops who occupied the place after the savage struggle looked no better than those they had conquered: ragged strips of uniform or often only the remnants of peasant clothing hung from their emaciated bodies. They were the troops of the Vietminh, 'The League for Vietnamese Independence'.

The head of this league was Ho Chi Minh, who had been provisionally elected president in 1945, but the return of the French army to Indo-China had at first prevented any further exercise of his office. Now he had beaten the French army with his band of Vietnamese peasants by brilliant tactics, thought out not by himself but by the Chinese general Lo Kwei-po.

Until 1949 the Vietminh had not been particularly successful in their struggle against the French, but in 1949 Mao Tse-tung came to power in China. Red Chinese troops occupied the northern border of Vietnam. And from then on, the Vietminh got what they needed: weapons, rice and military experts.

The Chinese general Lo Kwei-po took over supreme command of the Vietminh operations against France. The French sent in their air force. Only much later did they learn how hard the Vietminh guerrillas had been pressed by this air force, how difficult and insecure their position became, thanks to French air supremacy. The shrewd and experienced General Lo realised that the war could no longer be won by the Vietminh unless they managed to lure the main body of the French troops deep into the jungle. The French officers however were clever enough not to run this risk.

General Lo therefore decided—and later events can only be understood in this light—to attack the French not in Vietnam but in neighbouring Laos. Thousands of Vietnamese peasants were recruited to carry supplies, weapons and rice in endless convoys into the desolate mountains and valleys of Laos. In convoys many miles long they moved by night to avoid being seen by French reconnaissance planes. The alarm was only raised in the French garrisons in Laos when a strong Vietminh unit attacked the French positions about forty miles from the royal capital of Laos, Luang Prabang.

It was with great difficulty that the French managed to prevent the capital from falling into Vietminh hands. However, the Vietminh did not intend to capture Laos. General Lo's sole aim was to pin down the French in a hopeless jungle war and wipe them out. This time the French officers fell into his trap.

In assessing the likely French reaction, General Lo guessed correctly that they would *not* respond with the tactics of modern guerrilla warfare; here in Indo-China, they would employ the latest strategy learned in the Second World War. The rule, used by German and Allied alike, was to take the enemy from the rear by sending in a strong parachute unit. The first six battalions landed promptly on November 20, 1953, in the rear of the Vietminh in a hitherto insignificant village—Dien Bien Phu.

Six French battalions were too few for General Lo. So he let the Vietminh forces attack Luang Prabang in Laos twice more. On their second offensive, the Vietminh almost reached the boundary of the royal city of Laos. The French replied with the standard reaction: more and more troops to Dien Bien Phu to stop the Vietminh supply line from Vietnam, for in Laos the Vietminh was devoid of support or means of supply. Then when enough French forces were tied up in Dien Bien Phu, General Lo made his troops turn about and brought them back to Vietnam by forced march and surrounded the French in Dien Bien Phu. The French air force, successful though it had previously been, now proved too weak to break the ring around Dien Bien Phu. Its losses were too high, for the Vietminh had long learnt to shoot at the low-flying French with simple weapons like rifles and machine-guns (this is an art of guerrilla fighting which still worries the Americans today in Vietnam).

70

Dien Bien Phu became the Waterloo of the French in Indo-China. A modern army equipped with the latest weapons was beaten by a gang of coolies. Just as Mao Tse-tung after his Long March had thought his victory finally secure, so the Vietnamese communists believed themselves unbeatable. The West, hitherto represented by the French, was a paper tiger, just like those made of *papier mâché* set up at festivals in East Asia to be burnt for the pleasure of the spectators; a feeble thing, incapable of biting or scratching.

If Ho Chi Minh had had his way, he would have kept fighting on this wave of victory, driven the French further and occupied the whole of Vietnam and perhaps Laos and Cambodia, too, but it is thought that his Chinese military experts and his political and diplomatic advisers from the Soviet Union dissuaded him: the Chinese, because they knew to what a stroke of military luck they owed the victory at Dien Bien Phu; because they knew how weak, sick and underfed the Vietminh guerrillas were and for this reason feared a further struggle; the Russians, because they had been carrying out a peace offensive since Stalin's death, and perhaps, too, because they believed that in Asia the West might suffer a diplomatic defeat more easily than in Europe.

On July 21, 1954, France signed an agreement giving full recognition to the authority of the Vietminh, and thus to Ho Chi Minh, over North Vietnam as far as the 17th parallel. Other signatories of this treaty, besides France and Vietnam, were the Soviet Union and Britain. They all guaranteed the sovereignty of communist North Vietnam, the independence of the Kingdom of Laos lying to the west (which still belonged to the French Union), the sovereignty of Cambodia in the south and—temporarily—peace in South Vietnam.

The treaty laid down that general elections must be held in North as well as South Vietnam and that this vote should decide on the re-unification of Vietnam. It is said that Ho Chi Minh did not trust this clause in the treaty, but again it is said to have been the Chinese and the Russians who prevailed upon him to accept this stipulation. In French, British and American eyes, Vietnam had become a communist state with the conclusion of this treaty; not only the north of the country but also the south was obviously lost. France scarcely gave any support to South Vietnam's budding nationalist movement, the

Americans showed no interest because they did not wish to inherit France's problem and go through a second Dien Bien Phu.

If you talk today to Frenchmen who still live in Saigon they tell you with much vehemence and fury that at the time of Dien Bien Phu the war in Vietnam could have been won by France—if the USA had only brought her military power to France's aid then.

If you ask the Americans, who have heard this argument before, they will answer: 'We believe that. But that would have been a colonial war, an imperialist war, a war in which American soldiers would have fought not for the freedom of Vietnam but for its enslavement.'

By this they seek to emphasise that their present attack on Vietnam serves no imperialist purposes but aims to bring independence and freedom to South Vietnam and its non-communist neighbours.

While Ho Chi Minh secured his power in the north and set up a communist state, chaos reigned in the south. Private armies of different religious sects, especially those of the Cao Dais and the Hoa Hoas, fought each other and most of all they fought the 'government' troops which were still under French direction. The communist-inclined Vietminh was strongly represented in South Vietnam, but on the whole they kept apart from the fighting. Time, they thought, was on their side: according to the Geneva agreement there would soon be a plebiscite and the communists hoped that this would deliver South Vietnam into their hands without a struggle. They did not doubt that the North, being under strict communist supervision, and at least part of the South, would vote for reunification.

But they forgot to take Ngo Dinh Diem into account. Son of an imperial minister, Catholic, educated in French schools, and still living in a lay monastery in Belgium in 1953, after the fall of Dien Bien Phu he came back to his native Vietnam. After the Geneva agreement had been signed, the French puppet emperor, Bao Dai, who still had nominal sovereignty over South Vietnam, gave him the post of prime minister over the country to the south of the 17th parallel.

The Geneva agreement meant Diem to be the man to bury this shadowy state and prepare the general election leading to reunification with North Vietnam. Diem, however, had other ideas. Strongly influenced by the Catholics, who were being mercilessly persecuted by the communists in the north (one million Catholics had fled from the communists to South Vietnam), advised by his brother Ngo Dinh Nhu, and not least of all by the Catholic Church itself, whose right-hand man was Diem's second brother, Ngo Dinh Thuc, Archbishop of Hue, Diem decided to defy both the communists and the Geneva agreement with the pretext that order must first be established in South Vietnam.

Emperor Bao Dai stood in the way of order; ruling 'by the grace of France', he had utterly neglected the country for years. Prime Minister Diem staged a plebiscite, deposed the emperor and proclaimed himself president of the state, which he remained from 1955 to 1963.

During this time, Diem reorganised the South Vietnamese army, set up a semi-efficient government, filled all the important posts in the state with his faithful cronies, friends and relatives, and refused to countenance reunification under the communist aegis.

Diem had amazing success. He brought peace to South Vietnam, albeit a deceptive peace. His army appeared capable of being an efficient striking force, and the government—so it seemed—was in firm control of the country. Furthermore Diem succeeded in interesting the Americans, though no longer the French, in the preservation of a free, independent South Vietnam. The repeated warnings and sharp demands from the North Vietnamese and the Russians to carry out the general elections and reunification were dismissed by Diem. 'Free elections at any time, if you will guarantee that they will also be free in North Vietnam. It is obvious, however, that the communists will not carry out genuine free elections in North Vietnam, and under such conditions, I cannot hold an election in South Vietnam.'

This pleased the Americans, especially the then Secretary of State, John Foster Dulles. It was Dulles' policy never to allow an inch of ground to fall into communist hands where possible. Diem acquired unexpected American support. Ho Chi Minh looked on in fury as he saw his prey in South Vietnam elude him. This was the third time that he had been cheated of final victory. In 1945 the Chinese nationalists had contested his leadership by occupying North Vietnam, from 1946 to 1954 it had been the French and now Diem was defying him with the help of the Americans.

For the Americans, South Vietnam was something of a miracle. Out of this country which had been given up as lost in 1954, Diem had made an anti-communist 'bulwark'. South-East Asia—not only South

Vietnam but also Laos, Cambodia, Thailand, Malaya and finally even the Philippines—really might be protected from communism as long as South Vietnam could be kept free.

What the Americans obviously did not know because Diem did not tell them, although *he* knew, was the fact that the Vietminh, Ho Chi Minh's guerrilla forces, had only remained inactive in South Vietnam because they were still expecting peaceful reunification. When the Vietminh guerrillas realised in 1956 that Diem would not allow a general election to take place, they were ordered to regroup themselves and prepare for a decisive attack. This took them almost two years. The communists had concentrated too much on the purely political struggle, they had not replaced the weapons and food supplies discovered and confiscated by Diem's troops, had disbanded their regular units and had retained their headquarters as political centres only.

Now a new guerrilla army had to be recruited, organised, trained, armed and maintained. In two years this was done. Hundreds of Diem's government officials with posts in provincial or district towns were murdered. Hundreds of mayors who were loyal to the new regime, were 'sentenced to death and executed' by the guerrillas. The struggle for South Vietnam had begun. Diem, whose spies had always reported what was going on, played down the danger at first so as not to frighten off the Americans. Slowly but surely he made sure of increasing American aid for his troops, until America was irretrievably committed to the struggle for South Vietnam.

This explains, at least in part, the presence of America in South Vietnam today. It does not, however, come near to explaining the extraordinary initial success of the guerrillas, who from now on were called Vietcong, and it does not properly explain the turbulence of South Vietnamese internal politics, in which Buddhist monks burned themselves alive, President Diem was shot, and which led to a series of military insurrections in Saigon.

12

'ARE you looking for political parties in South Vietnam? Are you looking for political leaders? Are you looking for political issues? You can search for a long time and you won't find any of them. Oh, certainly there are thirty-five or forty registered parties. Each of them has a headquarters, where you will also find politicians. And they will all be talking of national issues. Do you want to know what I think of these parties? They are debating clubs with a membership of between twenty and fifty. The politicians at the head of them are people with extensive programmes, all beautifully democratic and very attractive, but the real aim of the entire programme is to bring this little group of politicians to power and thus to the state feeding-trough.'

The man who said this in Saigon is himself still a prominent politician in South Vietnam. He tried his best to explain to me at length how this political chaos had come about and why it still exists. I have already described some aspects of it: many of the best national politicians of Vietnam were put to death by the French police in the twenties and thirties. Others joined the Vietminh, in the forties, collaborated with the communists and were either converted to their cause or locked up and executed.

It was the Vietnamese nationalists who paid the highest price in blood all these years, but the nationalist Ngo Dinh Diem, president of South Vietnam from 1955 to 1963, dealt them their political death blow. For Diem was a dictator. He recognised only friends or enemies. Anyone who did not submit to his dictatorship was persecuted, exiled or, at best, politically extinguished. Those who bowed the knee, and they were not a few, were given offices and positions. So when the dictatorship of Diem was swept away in 1963, the dictator himself was not the only one to be murdered in the course of the operation and Madame Nhu, Diem's sister-in-law who had played so large a part in his state, was also not the only one who managed to flee the country. Diem himself had liquidated so many nationalists, but when he toppled from power the rest of the nationalists fell with him.

You can still meet enough people in Saigon today who will praise the good points of President Diem. Not only his strong hand, which South Vietnam doubtless needed in the chaotic times after the partition in 1954, but also Diem's ingenuity in building up the government and the army are praised. Diem wanted to give the country a new social and economic order, similar to that which General Chiang Kai-shek wanted in China. With his Decree No. 57 Diem even introduced a comprehensive land reform in South Vietnam. 'And from this land reform you can see clearly why Diem was bound to come to grief,' said my informant.

As I have already said, the Vietnamese villages have practised a system of communal land tenure since the very earliest times. Common ownership has usually extended to 20 per cent of the available arable land—quite a considerable area. Diem decreed that as a first step to land reform, these communal lands should be sold to the peasants. His aim also was to increase government revenue by this measure, so he ordered the fields to be sold by auction to the highest bidder and the money was to be handed over to the state.

The result was easy to predict: those who had enough fields could bid more than those who had none. Instead of the land being divided up among the landless peasants, the big estate owners would only become bigger. 'But that was not the worst,' my friend went on, 'for it was not the big landowners living in the villages who bought up the fields, but mainly speculators from the cities. And if there is anything the Vietnamese peasant cannot stand, it is the presence of city people in his village and strangers interfering in his affairs. Diem played right into the hands of the communists with this measure, for in Vietnam as in China there had existed from time immemorial a sort of rural defensive alliance, a union of peasants against the evils from the city: against the imperial tax-collectors, against the recruiting commissions from the army, against the officials who compelled them to hand over the harvest.'

These peasants regarded the sale of communal land to city speculators simply as a crime. And it was not hard to revive the traditional defensive alliance under Vietcong leadership. This intensified the guerrilla war, but it did not as yet endanger Diem's power. Diem made his greatest mistake (at least as far as his own life was concerned) in wanting to make the army his own special instrument of power. Generals and officers who did not submit to his authority and his secret police were removed. Furthermore these generals and officers, to a much greater degree than in other parts of the world, also had political, personal and even religious loyalties. The officers of a division stationed in one of the many provinces of South Vietnam could normally manage things the way they wished. Anyone wanting to practise politics in this province had to ally himself with the officers. If these officers were too subservient to Saigon or were dismissed, then the politicians and religious leaders behind these officers also lost their power. Thus every attack on the army also aroused political and religious opposition to Diem.

The history of the decline of Diem's personal power is long and complicated. One thing that is certain is that as early as 1962 Vietnamese air force officers tried to assassinate him by sending a bomber wing to attack the presidential palace in Saigon. The bombs hit their target and the palace has not yet been rebuilt, but Diem escaped with his life. This attempt at insurrection was followed by new purges.

Diem had by now antagonised everybody: the generals, the Buddhist monks who were strongly in league with the generals, opposition politicians and the largely communist-led students. The Buddhists were Diem's natural enemies, because he was a Catholic with a brother who was an archbishop and because he pursued a militant Catholic course in politics. The Buddhist fear, though not wholly founded, was that Diem would curtail their activities.

Added to this was the strong antagonism, to which I have already referred, between North and South in Vietnam. Like Ho Chi Minh, Diem was an Annamite from Central Vietnam, but in politics and character he belonged to North Vietnam. His followers, Tonkinese and Annamites, were Catholics who had fled from the North, whereas in general the Buddhists represented the southern part of Vietnam. All these tensions and forces contributed to bringing about Diem's fall.

'At the time it was said that the suicides [self-immolation by burning] of the Buddhists, the student demonstrations and the general unrest had caused Diem's downfall,' said my informant. 'But that is not true. There was and still is today only one force in South Vietnam which could do it: the Army.'

On November 2, 1963, the army struck. In the centre of Saigon they stormed the palace where Diem and his influential brother Nhu had taken shelter. Diem's bodyguard of trusted officers were no longer prepared to defend him. They defected to the army. Diem and Nhu were captured. Later it was said officially that while being brought to army headquarters in a closed car, they had 'succeeded in committing suicide'. The unofficial version was that they were both shot in the car.

Today in Saigon you can hear a third version, which probably comes nearest to the truth: Diem and Nhu were brought before the leader of the revolt, General Minh, and asked to sign a decree announcing their resignation. Not only did Diem and Nhu refuse, they also accused the officers present of treason and gave them warning that they would all be shot as soon as the tables were turned. This convinced the officers that they must forestall Diem and Nhu by shooting them first.

Later, the Americans were reproached for having deserted their ally Diem. The army would probably have given in to a strong American warning, because it was dependent on America for finance and equipment. It is not true, however, that the Americans simply left Diem in the lurch when his cause was lost. They had been watching Diem's autocratic behaviour uneasily for a long time and had given him repeated warnings. In the last year of his rule, Diem's relations with the Americans were particularly bad. When Diem used force against the Buddhists after the first attempted insurrection, the American Embassy opened its doors to the persecuted high priests and took them in, just as they had taken in Cardinal Mindszenty in Budapest. This was not only a humane act. It later proved to have also been a politically astute move, for the Buddhists of South Vietnam still remember these events.

Above all, Diem's fall taught America a lesson. From now on, it was decided, Vietnam's domestic politics would be left alone, but economic and military support would still be offered in accordance with the wishes of the government of the day.

This decision has since been repeatedly criticised, for one of the results of this American attitude was a constant succession of government crises. A tug-of-war began among the generals and between them and the few politicians left in South Vietnam.

The chief press officer of the South Vietnamese government, Mr Linh, described it to me in roughly the following words:

'In this country no one is in a position to do anything, except the Army. The political parties are practically non-existent or too weak. The Buddhists can only mobilise the mass of the people if they see definite proof that their institutions and religious freedom are in danger. The students are not a real political force. After Diem was overthrown it was only a question of which of the generals would be his successor. Since then, as you know, we have had several governments under the presidency of different generals. Even when we installed politicians as prime ministers, they could still act only according to the decisions of the army council of the time.

'For the past few years most of our strong generals have been in power. Each one believed he could rule without the assistance of the other generals. Believe me, I know them all, and they now realise that none of them can rule on his own. Since the fall of Diem we have had, to put it accurately, collective rule by the generals. And this group will remain in power until the land is at peace, till political parties are created on a permanent basis, till free elections have been carried out and the formation of a strong civilian cabinet is possible.'

Mr Linh could not say how much time was needed for such a development, but what he said about the group of generals is undoubtedly true. At the last insurrection, a young airman was given the post of Prime Minister by the generals—the thirty-five-year-old Air Vice-Marshal Nguyen Cao Ky. General Thieu was chosen as president of the state.

Ky is a Buddhist; Thieu a Catholic. If you examine the group of generals, you see that it consists not only of members of almost all religious communities, but what seemed more important to me, of members from all parts of Vietnam. Of course there are Buddhist protests against the Catholic president, Thieu, but the more the Buddhist Prime Minister Ky shows that he and not President Thieu is ruling the country, the quieter it becomes in the Buddhist camp.

'Anyway,' Mr Linh explained, 'even a strong Buddhist protest would

79

not prove an insuperable problem. We would simply have to remove the president and put another general from the group in the post. General Thieu would still remain in the group. And if Air Vice-Marshal Ky decided he preferred flying to ruling, he would still remain a member of the military junta, but would give up his post to another general. We don't reckon with any more violent revolts now.'

If this is true, there must be important reasons for it: since the last revolt, the American army has been actively engaged in the Vietnamese war, whereas before they were only there as military advisers. This intervention has raised the morale of the South Vietnamese army and of its officers and generals in particular. Whereas previously they had the feeling that they were fighting for a lost cause, they know today that they can no longer lose the war and their optimism even goes so far as to believe in a possible victory over the Vietcong.

Even the Americans are optimistic: 'With young Ky, a new order in Vietnam could be built up. He has great understanding and regard for democratic institutions. He is determined to stamp out corruption. He is keen to carry out reforms and therefore encourages the economic and social revolution. He is also the most co-operative Vietnamese government head to date towards the efforts of USOM and our own troops.' This, expressed with cautious optimism, is the American opinion on the present Vietnamese Prime Minister.

The problems which Ky has yet to deal with—quite apart from the struggle against the Vietcong—are enormous. The outcome of the struggle for Vietnam is to a very large extent dependent on whether the South Vietnamese government manages to deal with these problems.

13

In the tropics there is no dusk. In Vietnam too, the night remains dark till the stroke of six a.m. Life in Saigon, however, begins at four o'clock when the curfew ends. From then onwards the first taxis start circulating through the streets of the city; the drivers of the three-wheeled rickshaws call to the first passers-by; along the pavements gleam innumerable little charcoal stoves, on which breakfast is prepared for early risers. They are equivalent to the espresso bar for the poorer Vietnamese, for here they can get noodle soup for a few piastres.

Many of the people hastening through town are struggling to reach the large cross-country bus stations and the terminus of Air Vietnam. Most of them are carrying half a dozen bundles, baskets and packages. As soon as the buses arrive, they will be stormed by the passengers. The upper decks are piled six feet high with luggage. Jammed full like tins of sardines they then leave the city, at whose boundary the passengers must often get out for a police check of their papers.

It is remarkable how many different place-names these buses give as their destinations. Many lie at a distance of 60, 100 or 150 miles from Saigon. This did not fit into the picture that I had of Vietnam. Weren't the cross-country roads in Vietnam permanently closed? Didn't the Vietcong control large areas, and wasn't there shooting everywhere?

'Which provinces are actually Vietcong territory?' was one of my first questions in Vietnam. 'Are there no maps where they are clearly marked?'

'There are plenty of maps, new ones are drawn every day,' was the answer. 'But three or four such maps would have to be published daily to keep up to date. Territorial control changes from hour to hour. There are always at least two maps: one to show who held what during the night and the same for the day.'

Even as a European or American you can often travel long distances on the roads in Vietnam and even through Vietcong territory. The Vietcong usually refrain from molesting buses. They do not wish to draw unnecessary attention to the places where their troops are concentrated, or to draw the assault troops of the government or the Americans upon them by a rash attack. On the other hand—and this is perhaps as decisive as it is amazing—neither the Vietcong nor the government troops are interested in disturbing the population. 'Both sides need the people, both sides depend on them. The Vietcong need the rice, the money and the recruits, and strictly speaking these are the three things the government needs too. As a result, both sides see to it that the peasant can till his fields in comparative peace, that local trade continues without interruption, that the peasants earn their money and if possible are not driven from their villages.'

I myself watched an operation carried out by the assault troops of the Vietnamese government, in which South Vietnamese paratroopers and the Vietcong were engaged in a massive gun battle; yet less than 200 yards from the scene of this fight, dozens of peasants were busy harvesting their rice. They behaved as if the battle were nothing to do with them, and both sides engaged in the fight were careful not to shoot in the direction of the peasants. Of course, this is not always so. There are battles where the whole of the surrounding area gets blown to pieces and there are cases when the civilian population suffers more casualties than the military.

But in spite of such incidents one would assume that in Vietnam the government on the whole continues to function, that the government rules in spite of the Vietcong. This assumption would not be too far wrong. In the government offices they explain that practically all the capitals of the forty-three provinces of South Vietnam are firmly in the hands of government troops, that more than 80 per cent of the 14-million-strong South Vietnamese population live in areas held by government troops. 'The Vietcong control a large part of the mountains and the jungle, but not the main arteries of Vietnam,' it is said.

Yet the administration functions very badly in South Vietnam and the government works inefficiently. 'There is a lack of civil servants, especially honest and good officials, and the numerous changes of government in the last years have not improved this stage of affairs.'

From the fall of President Diem in 1963 until the installation of

Nguyen Cao Ky, the average duration of a South Vietnamese government was seventy days. Each new government began with an administrative reform which chiefly consisted in getting rid of the trusted agents of the previous government and replacing them by their own. In the province of Gia Dinh six new Provincial Governors were installed in eighteen months. In none of the forty-three provinces is there a Governor who has been in office for more than two years. The district officials have generally been changed along with the Governor.

'That would not be so bad,' the government openly admits, 'if these Provincial Governors and officials were at least all patriots! The greatest problem which faces us in Vietnam is the fact that our people have so little national pride. There is no patriotism, no national consciousness. It was once there: once, many hundreds of years ago, when we were under Chinese rule, we knew our enemy and we were conscious of our national identity. Under the French, too, our revulsion against foreign tyranny united us. And today it is doubtless anti-communism which makes our army fight and our people, on the whole, support the government. They have, however, little respect for this government. They hardly know the president and the prime minister, and the ministers are completely unknown.'

As I have already said, there are in addition great regional, religious and other differences which split the population. Not only are the people in the South—formerly Cochin-China—opposed to the Annamites from Central Vietnam and the Tonkinese from North Vietnam, but all of them are united in hating the dozen mountain tribes that populate the vast area of the Highlands. Until recently they were officially addressed as 'You savages'. It was the Americans who two or three years ago first began to show an interest in these mountain people and to build villages for them with the help of USOM, to fortify these villages, to bring food and clothing and to found the first schools. Plei Me, which has been fought over with such ferocity, is one of these mountain settlements built by USOM.

The University of North Dakota sent a team of professors into the mountains of Vietnam to record the languages of these mountain people for the first time, to establish a grammar and so lay the foundations for the first textbooks. In the last three years alone, this team has established the fundamental elements of six such languages.

In addition to regional hatred there are religious quarrels. In Vietnam these are by no means confined to Buddhists and Catholics. Nominally there are two million Catholics in South Vietnam (including the million Catholic refugees from the North) and 80 per cent Buddhists, but it is remarkable how many different sects are lumped together as Buddhists. There are about two million of the large Cao Dai sect, who have their own pope. This sect honours several saints, which include Sun Yat-sen (the Chinese democratic revolutionary), Jesus Christ, Victor Hugo, Buddha and several others. The Cao Dai are one of the best-organised and most militant religious bodies in Vietnam. For a time they joined forces with the Vietcong because they wanted to fight the Catholic Diem. When Diem was overthrown by the army and put to death, the Cao Dai went over to the government and today are their most faithful followers.

Then there is the sect of the Hoa Hao, which represents something like a South Vietnam Buddhist Front organisation against the Buddhists from the North. It is not sufficient that the new Prime Minister of Vietnam, Air Vice-Marshal Ky, is a Buddhist. He is a Northern Buddhist, and the Hoa Hao do not like him, even though they have so far not been too vocal in their protests.

Above all South Vietnam is marked by a strong contrast between town and village. The town dweller in Vietnam has never had the slightest feeling for the villager. Traditionally he regards him as a beast of burden, born to slave in mud and dirt, whereas the town represents civilisation. There are very few Vietnamese who would ever spend their holidays in the country, and it is interesting that they seldom have any family connections in the villages. For generations the town dwellers have grown up in towns and the peasants in the village, without there having been a migration from the country to the town. Even now when there are so many refugees in Vietnam and these mainly peasants, these refugees do not want to remain in the towns but to get back to the country as quickly as possible.

Previous governments, especially Diem's, made the mistake of recruiting their officials in the town and sending them out to administer the villages. There they were not only an impediment to good administration, but a favourite target for the Vietcong who could easily rouse the village people against these alien, town-bred officials. It was the Americans who recognised the mistake and prevailed upon the government to break with the system and to switch to a form of local autonomy. These local administrative forces are only now being recruited and sent through school, but this should go a long way towards satisfying the villagers.

USOM has even begun a new programme, which interestingly enough has been sharply attacked by North Vietnamese broadcasting stations and newspapers. The programme is called: 'City Youth goes to the Village'. I have seen the buses in which secondary schoolboys and students were being taken from Saigon to the neighbouring villages. There they had to live with the village people and help them for one or two weeks by working on the land. Officially, of course, it is a government programme. The North Vietnamese broadcasting stations claim that it has been planned by the CIA, and this has provoked the Saigon newspapers into declaring that, 'If the CIA is really financing this programme, it will be the first time that the CIA has done anything sensible.'

The government's great obstacle is the inertia of the population—understandable enough after more than twenty-five years of war. And no one knows how many years of war they still have in front of them. The most active element in the population are the Catholic refugees from the North. Not only have they almost all been to French schools and are therefore better educated than the rest, but they find powerful support in their church and because they are refugees and have to build their lives anew, they are twice as industrious as the local population. This has added another and often dangerous contrast to all the existing ones in Vietnam, for these Catholics very quickly reach the top in almost every walk of life, which arouses anger in all strata of South Vietnamese society, who blame the government for the rise of the refugees.

Another difficult problem, perhaps the worst of all—if one can give an order of precedence to the difficulties in Vietnam—is corruption. In the past, in Asia as in many countries to this very day, it was natural that anyone taking on rank and office should also gain material advantages from their position. The centuries-old mandarin system introduced from China brought this attitude to South-East Asia.

Before this century brought radical modern ideas to Asia, the people had always assumed that the material privileges of government officials were part of the natural order. The French did not alter the system, for it assured them an obedient class of local officials. After the French came President Diem and his whole system of personal power was based on the bestowal of posts which brought material advantages. Corruption and nepotism were the pillars of his regime.

That corruption must be swept away is a completely new attitude, which has only been current in Vietnam for the past few years. Until then no government had succeeded in putting the idea into practice. The present prime minister, Ky, is trying to stamp out corruption. He has not hesitated to bring a number of petty officials to justice on charges of abuse of privilege and to put the culprits to death as an example to others. But even he, who had started so promisingly, soon weakened in his efforts in the face of mounting opposition from the officials.

As Ky himself comes from the army, he believes, probably with good reason, that he can find the most honest administrators among the officers and NCOs of the army, so Ky has begun to put military men into the senior and middle-grade administrative posts. (A policy which Mao Tse-tung has also used in China.) Here, however, Ky is faced with a new difficulty: his military administrators are generally honest, but they do not know very much about administration. 'I'm learning the job as I go along,' two Provincial Governors explained to me. One was a colonel, the other a major. They had been appointed by Ky just a few months previously. Thus the army in Vietnam is beginning to take over key positions not only in the struggle against the Vietcong and in the government, but also in the 'civil' service.

Those who look for the growth of a large political party place more and more hope in such a party being formed from the large number of army veterans. 'They have all been through the same training, the tough school of fighting the Vietcong, and in the army they have more political instruction than any other citizen. In any case they are better patriots,' I was told in Saigon. If South Vietnam is ever to have a democratic future, it will need a patriotic party to create a sense of national unity. But in view of all the differences and all the disunity, it is amazing that the government has managed to defy the communists for as long as ten years.

The outside world, which is deluged with war reports from Viet-

nam, is inclined to regard the war in this country as a dispute between
the Americans and the communists. In Saigon they hotly deny this
point of view. 'It is our war, a Vietnamese struggle for freedom
against communist imperialism,' the government press officer told me
in almost angry tones. 'And the backbone of this fight is the South
Vietnamese army,' he added emphatically.

14

WE drove with our convoy of jeeps into a village. A row of Vietnamese soldiers was sitting in the village square. A blackboard had been placed in front of them. A lieutenant was standing at this board and beside him a white-haired old man. He was the mayor of the village and he was explaining certain diagrams on the board.

'We are having a lesson,' said the officer, when I had been introduced to him. It was an unusual lesson. The soldiers were being familiarised with the village and its situation. They were learning who lived in what house, which fields belonged to whom, where the storehouses and barns were situated and what problems the villagers had in bringing in the harvest.

'This is something brand new in South Vietnam,' said the officer. It is a great innovation for the regular army to show friendship to civilians. The guerrillas of the Vietcong have done this for a long time, but it has not occurred to any South Vietnamese government since 1954 to counteract this most effective means of communist propaganda by any action on the part of the government troops.

'For a time the soldiers thought all peasants were their enemies. Our own propaganda was to blame for that; we trained our people to think that the Vietcong were simply everywhere, that any peasant in the fields might unexpectedly draw a gun or throw a hand grenade. We failed to realise that the mass of the people probably do not belong to the Vietcong and that it is always only a few individuals who are active guerrillas. We ourselves added to the army's mistrust of the country people. The result is that the peasants mistrust the army.'

The army is still not very popular with the peasants today. Their programme of re-education has only been running for a short time, renewed on American advice in imitation of the successfully proven methods of the Vietcong. 'Not because we previously thought any differently,' they say at JUSPAO, 'but simply because we did not even see the problem. For American soldiers, friendship with the civilian population is automatic, and for a long time it did not occur to us that here it was not the case.'

Otherwise the Americans speak of the South Vietnamese army with respect. 'If you ask me, it is one of the bravest armies in the world,' I was told by an American major who had been working as adviser with a South Vietnamese regiment for two years. 'These boys fight with furious determination. It's often uncanny how calmly they accept casualties and in spite of losses throw themselves back into the fight.'

Before I went to Vietnam I had been warned against going into battle with South Vietnamese troops. 'They're reckless,' I was told. 'They take too many risks.' But I was glad that I did not take this advice. I spent two days and a night with South Vietnamese troops in Vietcong country. We had a few American advisers with us. The relations between Vietnamese and Americans could not have been more cordial. 'We had to learn this job the hard way,' said one of the American officers. 'At first we thought that when working with the Vietnamese forces we would be as well supplied as we are in our own army: two huge rations daily which bridge the gap between scrambled eggs in the morning and steak at night.'

During my short stay with the Vietnamese army I saw American officers eating roasted grasshoppers and fried caterpillars. 'We simply eat everything that doesn't eat us.' Besides—I can attest this from my own experience—they are quite good.

In battle the Americans rely implicitly on their South Vietnamese allies. In the barrack mess-rooms there are plenty of stories of how Vietnamese have rescued their American advisers by pulling them out of hopeless positions at no matter what danger to themselves. However, the other side of the coin is that many an American operation has been betrayed to the Vietcong as soon as it was made known to the South Vietnamese liaison staff. The Vietcong obviously have agents at headquarters level.

For a time there was a lack of good NCOs and officers in the Vietnamese army. 'Their troops have always been brave,' I was told, 'but their units were often needlessly destroyed because the officers lacked professional training.' The situation has somewhat improved in the last years. Nearly all the senior officers of the South Vietnamese army whom I met had not only done strict training courses in their own country, but many of them had also been trained in the USA, in Korea, in the Philippines and in Australia.

The army is also proud of the fact that more than half of its recruits are volunteers. At present, the army consists of 550,000 men. In view of the enormous losses which it has had since 1958, this is an impressive figure. Every year it is reduced by 10 to 15 per cent through deaths and serious wounds, yet there are 270,000 volunteers in this army. However, the pride with which they quote this figure is not entirely justified, for many young men only volunteer for the army for protection. In spite of everything, they are better off in the army than in many areas where there is fighting, especially if they live there. Then they run the danger of being recruited as cannon fodder by the Vietcong.

Others join voluntarily because they stand to gain from doing so. Every 18-year-old Vietnamese is called up for the army. He has to serve for three years, then he is demobilised, despite the continuing war, for the country needs young people for industry too. If he waits until he is conscripted, then the authorities have it in their power to assign him to any fighting unit. If he volunteers, he can choose the unit himself, and not only the unit: he can decide for himself in which province he wants to serve, and even under which commander.

It is one of the characteristics of the Vietnamese that even in battle they want to stay near their families. The Vietcong often even take their families with them on a military operation. Voluntary enlistment at least assures drafting to one's home province. 'Compared with other armies, we have a very high number of deserters,' the Supreme Command admits, 'although only a very few go over to the other side. They do not leave the army just to take the risk of joining up with the Vietcong. They run away in order to return to their families.'

Nearly all these deserters are not volunteers but conscripts. For, as the volunteers have the right to choose where they will be posted, naturally the conscripts will be sent to those places where there are too few volunteers and thus separated from their families.

'We deal leniently with this kind of deserter. If they are discovered, they are handed over to the district military unit, get six weeks' detention and are then taken back into the army with new papers.' This measure in itself creates deserters, for the boy is then put into his district unit and thus achieves what he wanted by his desertion, namely to serve in his home province. Of course he runs a certain risk: by law, the penalty for desertion is death by execution and there are also commanders who abide by the law.

Today one assumes in Vietnam that every young man of military age has joined up of his own free will. The advantages of joining this way are too great for the young people to lose by waiting for a call-up. Not all those liable for military service have been properly registered, not everyone receives his call-up order on his eighteenth birthday, and in consequence those who do not volunteer are treated fairly severely. It is almost impossible for a Vietnamese to avoid being stopped for a check-up at least once every few days. There are too many police patrols examining identity papers to find possible Vietcong infiltrators. Very rarely do these police checks actually catch a Vietcong, but they very often catch young men with no demobilisation papers from the army. They are 'recruited' at once, which means they are immediately brought under police guard to the nearest barracks. In Vietnamese official language this is called 'mobilisation on the spot'. Highly trained specialists such as economists, university teachers, technicians and civilian doctors are not infrequently victims of this 'mobilisation on the spot' if they do not have their certificate of exemption with them, or if a district commander decides to regard these papers as invalid.

The South Vietnamese army has not infrequently been heavily criticised in the foreign press for its ruthless behaviour towards its own civilian population, and especially towards the enemy. Until recently the ordinary people received little or no help from the army, whilst for a long time the army saw in every peasant a possible member of the Vietcong. In this way hundreds of peasants, even women, were taken into custody by the army and interrogated for days to find out whether they belonged to the Vietcong. This interrogation was often carried out in an 'incorrect' manner.

Prisoners from the Vietcong were given far worse treatment. In obedience to their orders, Vietcong prisoners refused to give information about their own units. It is extremely important in this partisan war for government troops to learn where the enemy is and what his intentions are. As a result district commanders often ordered prisoners to be tortured. I would not be surprised if this still goes on.

'It is a completely pitiless war,' a Vietnamese officer said to me. 'One sentence from the mouth of a prisoner can save the lives of hundreds of our comrades. It takes a lot to resist the temptation of extracting the information by any means possible; besides, the Vietcong do exactly the same to our prisoners.' He quickly added that these methods of treating prisoners have been forbidden and by law are liable to punishment, but Saigon is very far away when you are fighting in the jungle. When American advisers are employed, they have strict orders to prevent such behaviour by government troops. The Americans are at pains to bring the war back within the rules of the Geneva Convention. It is unbearable to them that American prisoners should continue to be tortured by the Vietcong.

The Vietcong are cunning. If they hear that government troops have mishandled prisoners or that Vietcong leaders have been shot by government troops as 'traitors to their country', they avenge themselves not on government soldiers but on American prisoners. For each Vietcong fighter that is tried and executed by the government the Vietcong kill an American officer prisoner.

The Vietcong broadcasting station which calls itself 'Radio Liberation' and operates from North Vietnam promptly reports the names of the condemned and executed Americans. The Vietcong reckons on the Americans protesting about this to the Vietnamese government, to prevent further torturing and execution of Vietcong prisoners. The Americans emphasise that in spite of these painful losses, they do not attempt to influence the decisions of the South Vietnamese courts martial, yet I have myself witnessed the great unease which prevails in all American organisations when the Vietnamese morning papers report that more Vietcong leaders have been executed as traitors. 'Now it will be one of our guys' turn again,' was the bitter remark.

The army of the Vietnamese government has borne the chief burden of the war since 1958. The USA has provided this army with weapons, instructors and advisers, but the fighting was done by Vietnamese troops whose political and psychological support from their government has been virtually non-existent. These governments seemed to do everything to antagonise the people of Vietnam and hence to antagonise the army. Through lack of economic and social reforms, the peasants were driven into the Vietcong army. Hatred of communism must be very strong among these people to have kept them going for so long in such a thankless struggle. In 1964 the government's neglect of political training and psychological warfare led to severe demoralisation among the troops. They fought on, but by 1965 they would no longer have been in a position to stand up to Vietcong pressure.

This situation and some crucial errors made by the Vietcong and the North Vietnamese government influenced President Johnson in July 1965 to do something which until then the USA had wished to avoid at all costs: the regular dispatch of American units to Vietnam. It had long been a firm rule in the Pentagon and in the White House never again to be committed to a land war in Asia with conventional weapons. No second Korea!

In July 1965, however, Washington had no further choice: only regular American units could stabilise the situation in Vietnam, perhaps even alter it decisively. The US Army might not win the war, but it would be unlikely to lose it.

15

'TIGER 5, Tiger 5 calling Puma 2, Puma 2' crackled the steady voice from one of the dozen two-way walkie-talkie sets in the command post of the American 1st Cavalry Division. In the same level tone one of the officers on duty relayed the orders over another network: 'Puma 2, Puma 2 calling Weasel 1, Weasel 1....'

Fifteen minutes later, thirty of the latest jet bombers were flying over a particular map reference in the Highlands of Vietnam. Hundreds of rocket bombs, containers of napalm and thousands of shells from the aircraft cannons were beating down on this target. An American patrol was hiding in this area. Fifteen minutes before, it had fallen into a Vietcong ambush. Fifteen minutes before, one of the soldiers had turned the knob on his radio set to 'Transmit': 'Tiger 5, Tiger 5....'

The immediate use of air support was only to pin down the Vietcong and relieve the pressure on the American patrol. The aircraft circled round this point until a black cloud appeared on the horizon; some dozens of helicopters of the 1st Cavalry Division. The first wave of these helicopters reached the map reference. Once again the patrol on the ground shot off its flares and smoke signals to show the helicopters exactly where it was situated. Quick as lightning the helicopters hovered down to the precise spot.

There was another hail of steel and fire as each of the helicopters fired its air-to-ground rockets, serving to check the Vietcong anti-aircraft fire. While the black clouds from the rocket detonations were still smoking up through the jungle treetops, heavily weighted nylon rope ladders were thrown from the helicopters. The weights smashed through the branches of the trees, through the top of the jungle undergrowth and reached the ground. While they were still falling the first American soldiers were beginning to slide down to the ground

94

on these ladders, like trapeze artists in a circus. The sequence of action was almost too rapid to follow: the ladders were being drawn up again, the first wave of helicopters was already pulling out while the next wave was hovering over the battle area with a deafening beat of rotors. In twenty minutes thousands of men from the Cavalry Division had landed in the rear of the enemy. Should it be necessary, 'Tiger 5' could call on thousands more men from 'Puma 2'.

At An Keh, in the middle of the Vietnamese Highlands, where the Vietcong have not met an enemy in twenty years, where neither French nor South Vietnamese troops have ever dared to venture, the Americans have moved in. Some hundreds of helicopters, many of which carry ninety-six men, flew in to attack An Keh. Not only did they bring a whole division into the jungle in one day, but they also delivered heavy artillery for this division. Here in the Highlands, where the Vietcong's heaviest weapon is a little portable trench mortar, the Americans brought heavy howitzers into position.

While the troops pressed back the Vietcong in heavy hand-to-hand fighting, giant bulldozers, likewise brought down by the airborne cavalry, were clearing the jungle and laying down an emergency airstrip. On the evening of the same day, the first supply planes could already land in the jungle.

Up at the front the most lethal modern weapons were in action and squadrons of fighter-bombers in more than 600 raids a day were unloading hundreds of tons of bombs and rockets. Out in the bush dozens of walkie-talkies were in use. Every little squad was linked with the neighbouring one by radio. If it fell into an ambush, it could immediately call for help.

Over the battle area one aeroplane was circling at a great height; no one except the commanding officers knew its mission. In this plane, a C-30 transport machine, there was a unit which the Americans call the ABCCC—Airborne Battle Control and Command Center. The technical equipment of this aeroplane is worth two and a half million dollars. Inside it sit officers in front of several television screens. A series of detailed maps appear on these screens showing the movements, one might almost say, of each individual American soldier. The information is transmitted to the flying command post and there, up in the sky, orders are worked out for the individual platoons. Computers help the officers to reach the right decisions, which are then transmitted by radio to the fighting troops.

The ABCCC is not only in touch with the ground; it is permanently linked with the helicopter bases, with the airfields from which the combat planes and fighter-bombers operate, with the aircraft carriers in the China Sea, with General Headquarters in Saigon, with reconnaissance planes and even with meteorological aircraft.

The flying command-post directs the air strikes and decides on the movement of supplies. It receives continuous news of the movements of the Vietcong from reconnaissance planes and the flying meteorological stations forecast the weather over the field of battle for hours ahead.

The flow of this information does not even stop at night. The American reconnaissance planes switch on an apparatus that the soldiers call 'Tipsy 53'. It is an apparatus that works with infra-red rays —rays which sweep the ground, rays which pierce the thickest clouds, the densest fog and the darkest night. They are rays which can distinguish vastly more than the human senses can. They distinguish trees from men, rifles from rice sacks, rucksacks from trench mortars.

When these rays have once caught the supply convoys of the Vietcong, they do not let them go. As prisoners from the Vietcong have said, it is often these rays which harass the Vietcong most sorely. In the middle of the night, in the middle of a tropical storm, under conditions in which the Vietcong always used to feel themselves completely safe, the American air force attacks them.

The Vietcong are not only afraid of rockets and napalm bombs and aircraft cannon shells. It is above all the American rifles which have inflicted heavy losses on the Vietcong. This newest American rifle—every U S soldier in Vietnam carries one—fires bullets with the effect of shells. Without even hitting the enemy it is enough if one of these shells strikes the ground two yards away from him, and the result at this distance is terrible. I have seen Vietcong snipers open fire on American troops who retaliated with 25 rounds per rifle in a few seconds: the trees were stripped of their foliage, the snipers swept away.

This is only one example of the fire-power which the Americans can bring to bear in Vietnam. The American command, however, knows very well that fire-power alone is not decisive. It helps to spare the lives of the greatest possible number of American soldiers, yet first and foremost it is the fighting spirit and skill of the soldiers themselves which count. Of course, every one of these soldiers is inoculated against every possible disease, he gets his anti-malaria pills daily, and by deliberate exposure for two weeks has been made immune to the bacteria which attack the intestines of white people. Even their uniforms and underwear are washed twice weekly by flying laundries. Above all there is an inexhaustible supply service behind each American soldier. Although it is made as easy as possible for these troops to keep alive in battle, neither fire-power nor supplies, nourishment and care can replace fighting spirit. This fighting spirit is perhaps the most surprising element of the American action in Vietnam.

'The Vietcong?' the American soldier who has just come from battle glances back to the jungle's edge. 'You want to know what I think of the Vietcong? They're brave men, but usually lousy marksmen—good soldiers but mostly badly trained.'

The fight with the Vietcong is a great game of cowboys and Indians, if one may use this expression for such a grim affair. And something has come about which has often puzzled even the experts: the American soldier has measured up not only to jungle warfare but also to partisan tactics. After several months' experience of fighting, the Americans have given up operating from fixed bases. 'I believe our Commander-in-Chief, General Westmoreland, keeps a picture of General Giap in front of him.' (Giap is Commander-in-Chief of the North Vietnamese troops and is, it is believed, Commander of the Vietcong.) 'The orders we get are exactly Vietcong tactics,' explained one of the U S officers. 'We don't wait any more to find out where and how the Vietcong are going to appear. We have gone over to the offensive. Our soldiers jump right into Vietcong territory, combing the jungle. He is just as likely to be taken by surprise as we are.'

Yet there exists a considerable discrepancy between the optimism one finds among the troops in the field and the opinions of those with longer fighting experience in Vietnam. 'Did you ask how long those soldiers you spoke to had been in Vietnam?' asked an American officer who has spent years in Vietnam as an adviser. Yes, I had. They had all come to Vietnam a few months ago.

'There you have it,' said the officer. 'Sure these troops use completely different tactics today and can do far more than we could with our South Vietnamese units all these past years. So they feel their military superiority. But in time our troops will begin to notice that they are fighting against an enemy who comes back for more just when you think you have finally beaten him. Don't misunderstand me. Our superior equipment, the high standard of training of our troops, the strong air support, and all our technical aids will no doubt produce a decisive turn in military events. But this war cannot be won by military means alone.'

I understood what he meant. I had been in the jungle myself: a division can disappear in it like a needle in a haystack. The paths which the troops have to hack through this jungle may be only a yard away from a Vietcong convoy without the convoy being noticed. You can be walking over an underground headquarters of the Vietcong without knowing that in the next bamboo thicket there is the main entrance to an enormous tunnel, without noticing that the tree in front of you is hollow and serves as an air shaft. How can you end such a war by conventional military means?

'Ultimately, military action is only a means to an end,' I was told in the US Embassy at Saigon. 'The most important thing is that at last the heavily populated areas are safe, that the Vietcong can no longer concentrate in regimental force undetected, and that the communists can no longer win battles on ground of their own choosing. That is the first task of our troops.' Their aim is to create the military conditions for a political solution of the Vietnam question. 'And our troops will achieve this,' they state with an astonishing degree of assurance.

If the Americans are not counting on a final military victory, what, I wondered, makes them believe that one day they too will not suffer a Dien Bien Phu in Vietnam, a decisive defeat? 'We wholly exclude the possibility of a Dien Bien Phu,' claim the American military men in Vietnam.

16

'TODAY we lost six aircraft, two over South Vietnam, four over North Vietnam. Six were saved from the crew of eight. The other two are considered lost.' Hardly a day goes past without the spokesman of JUSPAO in Saigon having to make such a statement to the correspondents assembled there. The material losses of the Americans in Vietnam are relatively high. Considering the fact that the Vietcong possess neither fighter planes nor heavy anti-aircraft weapons, they shoot down a great number of American planes. Over North Vietnam too, in fact there especially, the Americans often lose their fastest and most modern aircraft by conventional anti-aircraft fire.

'As regards South Vietnam, the cause lies in our tactical methods. Our planes cannot fly too high but they also must not fly too low if they want to bring their armament to bear most effectively. The Vietcong have been very successful in shooting down our planes.'

I was told that as a training-aid the Vietcong tie dead birds to strings and pull them quickly from tree to tree and their soldiers practise hitting the target with their rifles. A man who can hit a bird can usually hit an aeroplane. 'If there are 50 or 100 men who can calculate the speed of an aeroplane and they fire off a volley from their rifles, this can often be more dangerous than a radar-directed anti-aircraft gun,' the experts say. The Vietcong's rifles are well suited as anti-aircraft defence against modern jet bombers. The Americans have to some extent been able to armour-plate the vulnerable parts of their helicopters, but this is not possible with fighter planes. A rifle bullet can shoot them down. In North Vietnam they shoot at planes with rifles too, but they also have modern radar-controlled anti-aircraft guns and ground-to-air missiles which they get from the Soviet Union.

'It would not be difficult to destroy these anti-aircraft batteries or the ground-to-air rocket sites in North Vietnam,' the Americans believe. 'But this would mean using rockets ourselves. At the moment, with our policy of only carrying out limited air attacks on North Vietnam, we make limited use of ship-borne missiles.'

It is nevertheless astounding that the Americans manage time and again to save the pilots of planes which have been shot down, even when they land by parachute in the middle of North Vietnam. To save one man even a squadron of jet planes and bombers may keep the countryside around the pilot under heavy fire for several hours on end, which keeps the enemy at arm's length until the helicopters can pick the man up. The fighting morale of the American soldiers and pilots can be attributed in no small measure to the enormous effort which is made to stand by each individual and rescue him.

Massive material and technological superiority answers the question as to whether the USA may not one day suffer a defeat on the pattern of Dien Bien Phu. The Americans in Vietnam are convinced that there can be no Dien Bien Phu for them. 'There has never yet been a final defeat in the history of the American army. It will not be defeated here either.' This saying has almost become a slogan.

In talking to American officers today, any reference to the defeat of the French in the Indo-Chinese war is discounted. 'There are no parallels between their war and ours,' these officers explain. 'The French soldier was here almost against the will of his own political leaders, certainly against the will of the greater part of the French people. The equipment France sent to her troops in Indo-China was not the best, nor was there enough of it. Home was far away. The feeling of holding a lost outpost was strongly prevalent among the troops. There was inadequate air support. The French objective was a false one, and was recognised as false by their troops: namely, to maintain a colonial regime, to win the war for the purpose of an eternal status quo. Finally, these troops fought with the tactics of the Second World War and failed to understand the nature of guerrilla warfare.'

That is the American assessment. They describe their own case as follows:

'Our soldiers know that all the USA has to offer is at their disposal; that the President, if need be, would send another million men and the whole of the American air force to get us out of here. What is more important—our people know that they are not here to fight a colonial war; that no one will ask them to stay in this country. We are fighting for our South Vietnamese allies. As soon as we succeed in checking the Vietcong menace sufficiently to allow the South Vietnamese to finish things off on their own, then we will withdraw.'

At the end of 1965, there were 200,000 American soldiers in Vietnam, plus another 27,000 sailors and airmen operating from the aircraft carriers, about 20,000 other ground troops and pilots of long-range bombers. The strength of the American army was due to reach 400,000 at the end of 1966. According to the calculations of American General Headquarters, this number of troops should have been sufficient to check the Vietcong with the numbers it had at the time. The strength of the communists had not been underestimated—at least in the last years. At the beginning of 1966, the numbers of the Vietcong were calculated at approximately 270,000 men counting all its regular, regional and partisan troops.

There used to be a theory that the partisan struggle could only be checked if about ten men were put against each Vietcong guerrilla, the reason for this high ratio being that the government troops and Americans must keep them out of the government-controlled areas, and thus had to be everywhere, whereas the Vietcong could concentrate its striking forces at specific points of its choice. At any moment it may relax its pressure in one province in order to carry out a successful attack with united forces at any other point. However, the initial successes of the American troops, and above all their offensive tactics have now led the military experts to the conclusion that the Vietcong can be beaten with a ratio of 5:1 or even 4:1. As the government army consists of 550,000 men and is to be strengthened to 750,000 the Americans had to increase their strength—as foreseen —up to 400,000 men in order to reach their goal.

'Of course these calculations will only be correct as long as we have to deal with the Vietcong alone,' I was told in Saigon. 'Should more regular North Vietnamese or even Chinese army units join the struggle, the position will be more difficult.'

In the meantime, many battles have shown that regular North Vietnamese troops are being sent to South Vietnam. It is obvious why this has come about: the Vietcong forces are no longer strong enough to resist the pressure of the South Vietnamese army and the Americans. This was expected in Saigon: 'If and when things begin to go badly for the Vietcong we can expect to see extra efforts being made by the North Vietnamese.'

Yet, quite apart from the military task which faces the US Army, another important aspect of the war should not be overlooked: Vietnam has become an active service training area for the Americans, the testing ground for many of their most modern weapons, a trial of skill for hundreds of thousands of their officers and soldiers. Here they gain experience in fighting which no sandtable games or manœuvres, however realistic they may be, could provide. The armaments industry receives data from Vietnam, which in the event of a large-scale war will prove invaluable. To the surprise of armaments experts, aircraft, rockets, guns and small arms which were regarded as out of date stand the test of use in battle, whilst other equipment, hitherto considered far superior, reveals serious faults.

Furthermore, American officers who do not volunteer for the war in Vietnam must reckon on falling behind in their promotion, and understandably so, for they will lack fighting experience. The officer corps of other great armies in the world gained their most recent experience of fighting in the Second World War. In the professional sense, the Americans are 'envied' by other armies for their chance to give their officers battle experience in Vietnam.

It is astonishing that the Vietcong seem still not to have assessed the nature of their opponent. The tactics they use against the Americans are the same as those formerly employed against the French. They lie in ambush and try to draw large American units into indefensible positions, into a Dien Bien Phu in fact. And they are confused when a division lands in their rear. Today the Americans wait for Vietcong ambushes. 'That is almost the surest way of getting hold of the Vietcong and coming to grips with them,' I was told.

Wherever the Americans have gone into action, their superiority has greatly raised the morale of the South Vietnamese government troops and also of the civilian population. 'In this country, which has been a battleground for so long, the people have only one wish: to live in security and to be on the stronger side,' the South Vietnamese will tell you. 'In 1965 it looked as if the Vietcong would be the stronger, as if they could guarantee the country's security. Now the tables have been turned. Even the information about the Vietcong which we get from civilians has trebled in the last months. There could be no surer sign of the change in people's sympathies.'

I visited a province in Vietnam in which there are not yet any regular American units, a province in which for the last seven years the whole burden of war has lain on the government troops alone and on the few American officers who have been advisers to them throughout all these years. In the radio room of the regimental commander the American officers had put a motto on the wall years before and it is still hanging there. It runs: 'We have done so much with so little for so long that we can do anything with nothing.'

One of these advisers who has been working here for years was standing beside me as I read the motto on the wall. 'The Marines are coming the day after tomorrow,' he said, indicating the motto with a gesture. From then, there will no longer be any question of whether he can continue to hold the advanced posts for which, along with the South Vietnamese troops, he has had so long and bloody a fight.

In Cam Ranh Bay, scarcely ninety-four miles from this post, the Americans have begun to build an entirely new harbour, a harbour whose only immediate purpose is to land supplies for a part of their army in Vietnam. Docks a hundred yards long are being towed right across the Pacific and anchored in Cam Ranh Bay, docks complete with cranes, warehouses, crew accommodation, kitchens, etc. Sixteen ships a day are unloaded at these docks. Within six weeks a new South Vietnamese town has grown up around Cam Ranh Bay, which already contains 20,000 Vietnamese inhabitants. The harbour of Saigon has become too small for the volume of American supplies. Whilst the rate of supplies in January 1965 was 65,000 tons per month, by the beginning of 1966 it had risen to 750,000 tons.

The construction of the harbour at Cam Ranh Bay will cost the Americans at least a hundred million dollars, little enough in comparison with the material used daily in Vietnam, which amounts to something like eighty million dollars. One single attack by a jet fighter costs fifteen thousand dollars alone, and they fly four to five hundred missions daily, to say nothing of all the other operations carried out by the US forces.

17

'OUR troops would not be here today if the Vietcong and its leaders
in North Vietnam had not made a number of serious mistakes,' a US
diplomat told me as I sat opposite him in the American Embassy in
Saigon. 'The first of these mistakes was when the Vietcong began
attacking American establishments in South Vietnam. Bombs on the
US Embassy, bombs on the houses of our military advisers, bombs on
USOM. The Vietcong made their second mistake in changing their
tactics. They began to attack in battalions and regiments and switched
from waging a purely guerrilla war to conventional warfare.'

The bombings claimed several victims among the US personnel in
Vietnam. There is nothing to which the public in the USA reacts more
violently than the killing of American citizens abroad. Only after these
attacks could President Johnson count on widespread support from
public opinion and only in July 1965 did he finally decide to send
regular US divisions to Vietnam. For the first time there was full
agreement among the American generals that the Vietcong could be
fought by regular troops at all. For the Vietcong had begun to operate
in large units; they were no longer invisible and had chosen to fight
in the open.

There are no effects without a cause. The Vietcong made both
mistakes because they thought they were in the last stage of their
struggle in South Vietnam. The extraordinary success of their troops
was due in no small measure to the failure of the South Vietnamese
government on the political and social fronts in 1964 and the beginning of 1965. The South Vietnamese army was demoralised. The
Americans, whose intervention the communists doubtless feared and
did not wish to provoke, had made no preparations during all this time
to enter the war in Vietnam with their own troops.

In Hanoi and Peking the possibility of direct American intervention was excluded. What was more obvious then than to order the Vietcong to close in for the decisive blow? Partisan units alone, however, are not enough to achieve a complete military victory. The objective now was to capture cities and decimate enemy divisions. The struggle against the French had only been decided by Dien Bien Phu, when almost all the communist units had joined together in a set-piece battle. The Vietcong were therefore directed to form themselves into battalions and regiments and to attack in forces of 2,000 to 3,000 men.

They were also advised to make visible demonstrations of American weakness by bombing the American Embassy and American installations. It was these tactics that created the conditions for direct American intervention.

At the beginning of 1965, North Vietnamese radio stations and Vietcong transmitters alike began and ended their broadcasts with the slogan: 'This is the year in which we will finally be victorious.' In August, after the arrival of the first American troops in Vietnam, the slogan was dropped from the programme. Instead, the North Vietnamese President, Ho Chi Minh, declared, 'Even if we must fight for ten, twenty or thirty years, we shall win.' This statement and many other signs have led the Americans to believe that they can gauge the way the communists are now thinking which is roughly thus: 'In Hanoi they hope that the Vietcong, in spite of its military weakness, can continue the fight long enough to make us see the hopelessness of our intervention. They also hope that public opinion in America will one day swing to the point where American parents and wives will start saying, 'End all this and bring our boys home'; that the taxpayer will rebel at further sacrifices for the war in Vietnam. They place their hopes on the next presidential election campaign. They hope that there will be a presidential candidate who will campaign under the slogan: 'I will bring the army home.'

This is the American estimate of the way their opponents are thinking. At the same time they do not underestimate the communists' military logic: 'What did the Long March of Mao Tse-tung teach the Chinese communists? If one holds out long enough, the strongest opponent can be worn down. What did the French struggle in Indo-China teach the North Vietnamese? If one refuses to let up and sends the most experienced troops into action at the critical moment, the opponent capitulates.'

They also think that they know the degree to which ideology colours the thinking of Asiatic communists: 'As long as North Vietnam and China themselves are not attacked, they can afford to continue this war. First of all, it is excellent propaganda for the communists. It allows them to denounce American aggression and imperialist war-mongering and thus to confirm China's view of America. It enables them to arouse sympathy in other countries of Asia, in Africa and even in Europe and America. 'Hands off Vietnam' and 'Stop the war in Vietnam' are simple but effective slogans. Thus they can also mobilise a section of world public opinion against us which would otherwise remain indifferent.

'There is the additional factor that by exploiting this issue the Chinese can also keep their quarrel with the Soviet Union on the boil. Look, say the Chinese, the Russians won't help North Vietnam, the Russians keep up discussions with the Americans and are even ready to make common cause with them.'

The self-assurance with which these arguments were expressed makes it clear that the Americans are not at a loss for answers. The Americans now see the Vietnamese war in the following terms: 'The communists are going to find themselves in trouble, because the war is beginning to show that guerrillas, until now regarded as unbeatable, are losing too many engagements. Of course they can still manage to infiltrate saboteurs and their snipers still pick off our men from ambush, but it will soon be obvious to the whole world that a great modern army, even in unfavourable geographic and climatic conditions, really is capable of defeating communist partisans. This realisation will be a serious blow to Chinese propaganda. What price their "paper tiger" theory then?'

'Have you,' I was asked by an American diplomat, 'read some of the articles published by the North Vietnamese and Chinese politicians? They themselves describe Vietnam as the test case which will prove that all the "oppressed" peoples of the world can beat off foreign "domination" by revolutionary wars of liberation. What happens, then, if they fail to beat us here? What if they are beaten in this war? The answer is that their theory would boomerang on the Chinese communists themselves. It would be an ideological defeat.

'China has threatened us for about the four hundredth time and announced for the hundredth time that she is about to rush to the aid of the fraternal North Vietnamese and defeat us. Where is this aid? Not only the North Vietnamese and the Vietcong but the whole of the rest of the world must be asking this question by now. Chinese reluctance to join in the fight hardly seems to square with their description of us as a "paper tiger". The present situation in Vietnam is proof that China is ready to fight to the last Vietnamese, but not to risk her own security.'

The Chinese attack may yet come, possibly for the very reason that China is now beginning to lose face in Asia. I was definitely able to sense this on my journey through several Asian countries. No continent reacts so quickly to power and success as Asia. On my last Asian trip, a year earlier, Asia was still convinced of China's invincibility. Pakistan aligned herself with China; Soekarno even took Indonesia out of the UN to please China; Burma wanted to have nothing more to do with the West; Prince Sihanouk of Cambodia broke off relations with the USA and banished all Americans from his country; the Laotian government was in a dilemma over its allegiance and even in the Philippines and Japan voices were heard demanding a reorientation of their countries' foreign policy.

China exploited these tendencies to the full, but she was equally aware of the threat to her image in Asia that could result from direct American intervention in Vietnam. This was the test which, as I knew from personal observation, Peking had always wanted to avoid: the test of whether the American tiger really was made of paper. Because, in contrast to their speeches, Chinese politicians have always acted with great caution. Since Korea they have steered clear of any policy which might provoke a direct military confrontation between China and the USA.

Then American troops landed on the Asian mainland, at the very gates of China and in a country about to be brought firmly and finally into the Chinese orbit. American planes were bombing North Vietnam, a country which had a military alliance with China, making China virtually compelled to intervene on North Vietnam's behalf. This time, however, the Americans had made it quite clear that if Chinese troops were employed the conflict would not be limited to non-Chinese territory as it had been in Korea. Direct intervention by Chinese troops

107

would be answered by a direct American attack on China. Peking is therefore running a very great risk.

China has recently attempted to raise her prestige elsewhere in Asia, notably during the short Indo-Pakistani war, but with the same negative results. Peking issued an ultimatum to India, extended it for three days and finished up by saying that Chinese intervention was unnecessary because the Indians had complied with the ultimatum.

There can scarcely be any doubt now that the bloody uprising in Indonesia was inspired by pro-Chinese communists, the probable aim being to bring off an impressive *coup* at another point in Asia to offset the threatening new situation in Vietnam, but like the Sino-Indian incident, this attempted revolution was a failure.

There have been slight signs from China that certain of her leaders wanted to bring about a change of course in her foreign policy. Premier Chou En-lai and foreign minister Chen Yi are thought to belong to this group. They are said to have been called to order on October 1, 1965, at an extended session of the Central Committee of the CPC in Peking, to have been overruled and forced to concur with an even tougher line in foreign policy. Once again the spirit of the Long March has won the day, the spirit of rock-hard resistance against which the opponent will wear himself down until he gives up. Then, however, came another blow—the clearly expressed rejection of China's policy at the preliminary talks of the Afro-Asian summit conference, which led to the cancellation of the conference itself. China's pretensions to be the spokesman of the Afro-Asian bloc suffered a heavy blow.

It is unlikely that the Americans foresaw all this when they decided to intervene in Vietnam; indeed, my impression was that this development surprised the Americans most of all. They had counted on the Afro-Asian countries uttering a howl of protest when US troops marched into Vietnam. There is a protest movement in the USA itself, but in Asia America won an unexpected amount of open sympathy. Some of the Asian governments felt that it was high time to put a stop to China's aggressive policy, an opinion which possibly is even shared in Moscow.

18

BASICALLY the Vietcong are supplied from the North by two channels—the sea route down the coast and the land route known as the Ho Chi Minh Trail. The seaborne supply traffic is constantly being harried by the famous 'Junk Fleet'—Vietnamese craft fitted with outboard motors and guns and led by American marine and naval advisers. The Junk Fleet's operations are so effective that more and more of the Vietcong's supplies are being sent by the Ho Chi Minh trail.

The trail is quite easily detectable from the air in the places where it is not completely overgrown by the jungle. It is much more than a trail; it consists of an arterial system of parallel linked paths, tracks and even roads, all leading roughly from the Dien Bien Phu region across the North Vietnamese frontier into Laos, southward along the Laotian side of the border with South Vietnam until the trail breaks off into a dozen sub-trails leading into different South Vietnamese provinces.

The Vietcong convoys move along this network at night carrying sacks of rice, rifles, machine-guns, mortars and ammunition on their backs. Occasionally the Laotian air force attacks the trail, but along one sixty-two-mile section it is even used by lorry convoys. But the Americans say that the volume of supplies passed down the trail is not so significant. There is a lot of talk, and differences of opinion, about this in Vientiane, capital of Laos, but it is no secret that across-the-lines communication is relatively free in Vientiane: not only do Americans talk to Russians, but Russians to North Vietnamese, the latter to Chinese and vice versa.

Certainly the Americans want to confine the war to Vietnam and would go to considerable pains to avoid North Vietnamese infiltration into Laos. For the same reasons of 'confinement' they have so far carefully avoided attacking Hanoi and other northern industrial centres, the port of Haiphong and the dams and irrigation works of the Red River delta—the most sensitive targets in North Vietnam. One explanation—though founded on little more than intelligent supposition —would be a secret exchange between the Americans and the Russians. It is quite obvious that massive American air attacks on Hanoi, Haiphong and the ricefields of the Red River delta would rapidly bring North Vietnam to the brink of economic and political collapse. The result would be a call for help to China, to which China could only respond with a maximum of military aid and perhaps with the dispatch of regular Chinese troops.

In such an event, as I was personally told by the Chinese foreign minister, Marshal Chen Yi, China would extend the field of action over as wide an area of South-East Asia as possible. The war would then spread not only to Laos but probably to Cambodia and Thailand as well; only by this means could the Chinese fully exploit their one advantage over the Americans—their numerical superiority.

So far it has been in the interest of all sides to avoid increased escalation. The Americans have made it clear what their response would be. Since they would be hard pressed to check a major Chinese advance into South-East Asia (the Chinese army is reckoned to be three and a half million strong) they would attack China herself from the air, beginning with heavy air raids on key industrial and transportation centres and probably leading up to an attack on China's nuclear plant. This would mean the probability of seeing all or most of her laborious industrial growth of the past fifteen years, including her atomic centre, smashed to pieces in a few days. It is, above all, this prospect which restrains China from more active intervention in Vietnam.

Even this interpretation, however, is incomplete as it leaves out the other two main parties to the conflict—the Soviet Union and North Vietnam.

Most experts agree that the North Vietnamese would be most reluctant to call in Chinese troops. In 1965, before the 'cultural revolution' in China, the North Vietnamese press was staging a big campaign under the slogan: 'Love your Chinese brothers.' The very fact that such a campaign was thought necessary was evidence that they did not yet love their Chinese brothers quite enough.

The Vietnamese have never been very fond of the Chinese. Vietnam and China in the past have been constantly at war. China has made repeated efforts throughout her history to conquer Vietnam or at least to reduce her to tributary status. In keeping Chinese troops out of North Vietnam, therefore, Ho Chi Minh is to some extent conforming to a traditional national policy of independence of Peking, a factor of which the Americans must be aware. The Russians, too, are doing what they can to help Ho Chi Minh counteract excessive Chinese influence by supporting him with arms, food, money and diplomatic advice. Nevertheless if the Americans were to step up their attacks on North Vietnam to a dangerous extent, Ho Chi Minh would have no alternative to putting his country's fate entirely into Chinese hands.

In Saigon I enquired into the methods used in carrying out the American bombing raids on North Vietnam and I was astounded by the care used to ensure that wherever possible no American raid oversteps the political danger mark. Reconnaissance planes bring in target data from flights over North Vietnam, which are analysed on the spot. (Probably aboard one of the large aircraft carriers from which the American bombers operate against North Vietnam.) From there the analyses are sent by radio and television to Pacific Command Headquarters in Hawaii, where they are studied and checked again. Hawaii then retransmits its evaluation of the data straight to Washington. There the Pentagon passes the target data to the National Security Council; this is the body which, in consultation with State Department advisers, decides which targets in North Vietnam can be bombed.

If the decision is confirmed the orders come back from Washington via the Pentagon and Pacific Command to the aircraft carriers in the China Sea. The bomber pilots are then briefed both by their commanders and by political advisers before they set out on the raid. One might expect this complicated process to take several days; in fact orders from Washington usually take no more than two or three hours to come back to Saigon. This elaborate care is exercised in order to leave the North Vietnamese government the option of suspending aid to the Vietcong and sitting down round the conference table.

American diplomats openly admit that other considerations play a part; it is no secret that both the USA and the USSR are united in wanting to keep China out of the Vietnamese war, but beyond this no one can be sure how the Soviet Union would react if the USA were compelled to attack mainland China. This could be the crux, the point at which this local war might escalate into all-out nuclear conflict and which the Russians and the Americans want to avoid at all costs.

Behind the scenes in Vietnam a very delicate diplomatic game is being played. The moves in this game affect the day-to-day conduct of American military operations, especially those of the US Air Force against North Vietnam; whilst American and South Vietnamese troops are fighting the Vietcong with no holds barred the spread of the war is being resisted in order to give the North Vietnamese a chance to disengage and negotiate.

'We have never suggested,' say the Americans in Saigon, 'that we have any desire to attack or unseat the communist government in Hanoi. We want Ho Chi Minh, the Russians and the Chinese to realise that we are not concerned with redrawing the political map in South-East Asia, simply with a confirmation of the status quo—which means preventing South Vietnam from becoming a communist state.'

This view of American policy is liable to be modified when one hears it formulated in Washington, where it is expressed in rather more realistic terms: 'The spread of communism by force of arms must be prevented in Asia, just as it was prevented in Europe. Somewhere we have to draw the line. In Europe we drew it by means of NATO; in Asia our problem is that we may be trying to draw it too late. We are now faced with the choice of either drawing it on the Thailand frontier and the coastlines of Japan and the Philippines or at the point where communism has most recently attempted an armed takeover, namely Vietnam.

'We have decided to draw the line at that point—and now. This does not mean that we want to dragoon the non-aligned South-East Asian states into SEATO or any comparable organisation; we would be quite satisfied with a neutralisation of South-East Asia, provided it was genuine and there was no danger of its subversion by communism. We shall bless the day when we can withdraw from here, when a sound government can look after South Vietnam's affairs.'

How then can this war be ended and this goal reached?

19

'THE North Vietnamese are Vietnamese first and communists second.'
Thus spake Mr Linh, the South Vietnamese government's Chief of
Intelligence, in a talk lasting several hours that I had with him in
Saigon. He had several more unusual remarks in store for me. He said,
for instance, that elements of the communist-run 'National Liberation
Front', the political organisation behind the Vietcong, could well be
included in the negotiations for a South Vietnamese government after
a cease-fire. One might even visualise a parliamentary party emerging
from the National Liberation Front.

'Don't misunderstand me,' said Mr Linh; 'the Communist Party can
never again be allowed to function in this country. No one who has
tried to subvert law and order by force of arms has the right to freedom
of political activity. We believe, however, that the National Liberation
Front contains a number of moderate, progressive nationalist elements
within it who may welcome a chance to break away from their forced
alliance with the communists.'

The Americans in Saigon are prepared to take this point a step
further: 'We believe that there are more than a few genuine patriots
fighting in the ranks of the Vietcong. Before we began pressing them
really hard, the Vietcong were undoubtedly able to win over a number
of men of good will. Vietnam is going to need these people in the
future task of political and economic reconstruction.'

The long-term problem which most concerns Vietnamese and
Americans alike is whether they can succeed in building up a strong,
patriotic party of the centre as a counterbalance to a left-wing socialist
party formed from elements of the National Liberation Front. At
present there are far too many political splinter groups in South Viet-

nam to form such a party. There is too much divergence among the potential leaders, whether politicians, military men or religious leaders. This corresponds to the spirit of factionalism which seems an inbred characteristic in the Vietnamese: they tend to be religious or regional separatists lacking much sense of national cohesion.

Praiseworthy though this concern about an eventual political realignment in South Vietnam may be, I could not help feeling that the question of how to end the war was far more pressing and important. The Americans themselves say that the war cannot be won by military means alone, despite the superiority of the American troops. They pin their real hopes on the social and economic measures which I have already described. But they also realise that in this country, where thousands of square miles consist of jungle-clad uplands and the northern and western frontiers are virtually insecurable by patrolling, etc., it will be an impossible task to stamp out guerrilla activity altogether. The communists will always succeed in infiltrating small bands to sabotage, terrorise villagers and pick off government patrols. The war, therefore, can only be brought to an end by negotiating with the men who train these guerrillas and give them their orders. These men, the Americans believe, are to be found in Hanoi and are presumably strongly supported by China.

So it is questionable whether Hanoi can ever be brought to negotiate without Chinese consent. As matters stand at present, China is unlikely to give this. It would be too great a loss of prestige and would mean a deviation from their ideological line of 'continuation of the world revolution through national wars of liberation'.

There might, of course, be a change of policy in Peking. Another possibility is that with Soviet Russian help Hanoi might shake itself free from the material and ideological grip of China and adopt a more independent, perhaps even a Titoist, line of policy. Both these moves, however, seem improbable in the present state of affairs.

'If you ask me, this war will never be brought to an end,' I was told when I questioned one of the leading American authorities on South-East Asia. 'This war will simply wither away. The day will come in Hanoi when they realise that there is nothing to be gained in South Vietnam by military means. The results of sporadic guerrilla attacks will simply be outweighed by the damage suffered in North Vietnam from our air raids.

'We shall reach a point where they want the attacks stopped, just as we want the guerrilla raids stopped. These wishes, in my view, will not be expressed at a major international conference but more probably at discussions carried out through intermediaries in some third country. It may well be that neither side will make a public announcement of the cessation of hostilities; instead, operations by the US Air Force and the Vietcong will simply diminish from day to day until they peter out. Both sides, for the sake of prestige, will keep up the fiction that no agreement has been reached, but *de facto* peace will gradually return to Vietnam.'

When I raised objections to his hypothesis, my informant agreed. 'Naturally both sides will feel uneasy about ending the war in this way. World opinion will probably be suspicious about an undeclared armistice without great discussion and without a signed agreement. But any kind of conclusion to this war is better than none at all.' Of all the views that I have heard on a possible means of ending the Vietnamese war this one struck me as being especially interesting, because it was very Asiatic.

'The Vietcong,' he went on, 'would control some areas for a while and our troops too would stay on in Vietnam for a certain time. Discussions could then be held over a phased disbandment of Vietcong units parallel to the gradual withdrawal of American troops. However, everything will depend on how strong and how competent the South Vietnamese government is at this point.'

The South Vietnamese themselves have a totally different conception of the way the war may end. They believe, rightly or wrongly, that North Vietnam is keenly anxious to be rid of Chinese domination. They also believe that the North Vietnamese (by this they mean the Tonkinese) have ambitions to be an independent and influential power in South-East Asia, and they pin their hopes on a plan which the Americans, its authors, have been rather soft-pedalling lately. I refer to the 'Johnson Plan' for the pacification of South-East Asia.

President Johnson's proposal was to found an international development bank for South-East Asia, in which the USA and the USSR, and as many other countries as possible, would deposit large funds. The member countries would be North Vietnam, South Vietnam,

Laos, Cambodia, Thailand and possibly Malaysia and Burma. The bank would have a function similar to that performed in its time by the Marshall Plan in Europe: the joint economic development of the whole of South-East Asia. All member states would retain their sovereignty, each country would have its own form of government, whether communist or non-communist.

The bank would be neither the agent of the USA nor of the Soviet Union or of any other states. Its aim would be simply peace and prosperity instead of war, subversion and guerrilla infiltration. Individual member states could retain their military alliances with other countries if they wished—North Vietnam could keep her links with China and the USSR, Thailand with the USA. Equally, any member could be completely neutral and free of alliances, a choice which might be favoured by Laos and South Vietnam. The USA already has 1,000 million dollars put aside for this project. The Russians have not completely rejected the idea of the bank; their hesitancy is in any case understandable, as they could hardly endorse it without the concurrence of North Vietnam and they must also make sure of China's attitude.

Although American diplomats in Saigon are not too sanguine about the chances of this plan as a means of bringing about peace in Vietnam, it is regarded in South Vietnamese government circles as constructive and realistic. 'It would have considerable attraction.' I was told, 'for the North Vietnamese in particular. It is the only country in the region that has coal resources, the basic raw material for industrialisation. The Tonkinese and Annamites are also unusually hard-working and good organisers and have always had ambitions to play a leading role in South-East Asia. This might disturb the Laotians and Cambodians, and possibly the Thais, but if their sovereignty is fully guaranteed, as was the case under the Marshall Plan in Europe, these countries would hardly be in a position to object to the economic advantages accruing to a country that had the most to offer in the way of resources. North Vietnam, in fact, would become the leading economic partner in such a community.'

I remarked during this discussion that North Vietnam was nevertheless strictly a communist state which had hitherto given no cause for anyone to assume that it might be prepared to collaborate with its non-communist neighbours or with a largely American-financed development bank. Mr Linh's answer to this was that North Vietnam might well be forced to modify her attitude as a result of the ultimate outcome of the war. 'If you beat a dog,' he said, 'and drive it into a corner of the room where there is a hole, it will bolt through that hole.'

The 'hole' is the alternative way out which the Americans have been careful to create for North Vietnam. The US government repeats almost daily that its aim is not to conquer North Vietnam, that it has no wish to cripple the North Vietnamese economy or to harry the civilian population with bombing attacks, but merely to destroy the North Vietnamese bases and training grounds of the Vietcong.

Another significant feature of US strategy in Vietnam is the American refusal to form a joint US-South Vietnam supreme military command. A joint command would greatly improve operational planning and control of the war effort; one may therefore legitimately wonder why the Americans have so far avoided setting it up. The official American reply in Saigon is that any such move would turn the Vietnamese war into an American war. There is, however, another answer which the Americans are less willing to spell out: by forming a joint command, the Americans would be deprived of a vital degree of freedom of diplomatic action. If, for instance, Hanoi or the Vietcong were to make a peace offer, the USA would want to retain full liberty to negotiate. A South Vietnamese government might reject the peace proposals—and no one can tell what sort of government is likely to be in office when the moment comes. If the American troops in Vietnam were under the control of a joint command it would be far more difficult for the American leadership to propose a truce or to act in support of peace negotiations if the South Vietnamese General Staff were opposed to it.

Although these considerations relate to the future, it is encouraging that such intensive thought is being given to them because they are the main element in giving sense and purpose to the American intervention in Vietnam. For the moment, though, first things come first— the fight against the Vietcong, social and economic reforms on the home front.

In the last resort it is these twin operations which will decide whether and how the war is brought to an end and despite initial successes plenty of setbacks and a greater build-up of American military strength can be predicted before that aim is achieved.

20

'The Americans can't lose the war now'—that is what one hears in Saigon and Vientiane, in Bangkok and in Hong Kong, from nearly all diplomats accredited there. This opinion is even shared by the emissaries of the Eastern bloc.

Naturally the Americans are also firmly convinced that their troops will turn the tide of war in South Vietnam, although there are still some unknown factors in the equation. An attack by the regular North Vietnamese army along a broad front is one of these unknowns. Another is the attitude of China: will Peking really keep out of the war if one day it becomes obvious that the Vietcong are losing? The third unknown factor, however, is not to be found in Asia but in America itself.

The Americans in Saigon are disturbed at the increasing number of protests and demonstrations in America against the war in Vietnam. They believe that the American public is still not sufficiently well informed as to the why and wherefore of this war.

They also realise that the present engagement of the US Army in Vietnam is still not adequate to win the war. The despatch of a further 200,000 soldiers, bringing the total complement to approximately 600,000 troops in Vietnam is, according to military experts, a *sine qua non* for ending the war. To marshal such a force, however, the US government needs the support of public opinion in America. The question which faces the American public is harsh and simple: will this sacrifice achieve its goal, and is that goal worth the sacrifice?

There can hardly be any doubt today that an unconditional withdrawal by the USA would represent for America a defeat of world-wide significance. South-East Asia could no longer be saved from Chinese-style communism. After South Vietnam, Laos would fall; after Laos it would be Thailand's turn, and after Thailand neither

Burma nor Malaysia—probably not even India—would be able to hold their own. America's credibility as a protecting power would then be very much at stake in Africa and in Latin America.

Until July 1965 the USA might still have drawn a new 'boundary', making the line of defence against Asian communism not in South Vietnam but on the Thailand border. After the dispatch of her troops to South Vietnam, however, there is no more retreat for the Americans. Nor can they afford to abandon the war in Vietnam without bringing it to a decisive conclusion. The Vietcong and the so-called 'National Liberation Front' (the political cover organisation of the Vietcong) appear to have realised this even sooner than some people in the USA.

The Vietcong sent a diplomatic mission to Moscow some time ago. They will not allow themselves to be represented in the Soviet Union by the North Vietnamese. In this way they have underlined the fact that they wish to be, on the face of it at least, an autonomous South Vietnamese organisation. One of their representatives in Moscow is Nguyen Van Dong. Mr Dong spoke at a press conference in Helsinki. And he made two sensational announcements:

Relations between the Vietcong and China were very strained.

The Vietcong were ready to participate in peace talks without prior conditions.

On the first point, the Vietcong are certainly in a better position than far-away China to estimate how severe American pressure has already become in South Vietnam, and they certainly know better than the Chinese how long they will be able to withstand this pressure. Above all they are aware of the casualty rate sustained by the Vietcong in continuing the fight against such a well-armed opponent.

Understandably enough, the Vietcong are not anxious to bleed to death for the sake of China's foreign policy if there is any hope of ending the war without their own total extinction.

Van Dong's second pronouncement is implicit in this: 'Peace talks without conditions'—which would seem to indicate that the Vietcong would not insist on the withdrawal of the Americans from South Vietnam, but would be prepared to sit down at a conference table with the USA even if American troops were still operating in South Vietnam. But this is entirely contrary to the attitude adopted by the North Vietnamese and more especially by the Chinese.

North Vietnam has laid down four essential preconditions to peace talks:

The American troops must withdraw completely, their bases must be vacated and the American-South Vietnamese defensive alliance annulled;

Until the peaceful reunification of Vietnam, North and South Vietnam should form no military alliance with third parties and should permit no foreign troops on their soil;

The internal affairs of South Vietnam must be settled without outside interference by the South Vietnamese, on the lines of the programme of the 'National Liberation Front';

The peaceful reunification of North and South Vietnam should be accomplished by the people, without outside intervention.

These are the preliminary conditions stipulated by North Vietnam for peace talks. But Mr Dong, a representative of the 'National Liberation Front', a representative of the Vietcong, said very clearly in Helsinki that the Vietcong themselves no longer insisted on any conditions for peace talks.

This was further specifically emphasised by Mr Dong some days after his press conference when he denied that he had talked about bad relations between the Vietcong and China. But that was all that was contained in his denial. He did not deny that the Vietcong were prepared to negotiate with the Americans while their troops were still in South Vietnam.

The Americans have been criticised, especially by Jugoslavia and other members of the Eastern bloc, for wanting to bring about peace in Vietnam through negotiations with North Vietnam and even with China instead of by direct talks with the Vietcong. According to Jugoslavia, the USA should above all disregard the Chinese. They should recognise the Vietcong as an independent, national South Vietnamese organisation and negotiate with them. It is probable that this view is now also shared by the Soviets.

So far the USA has rejected this approach. 'Any attempt to talk with the Vietcong alone would probably result in the collapse of South Vietnamese resistance and probably even of the South Vietnamese government,' was the reply made by Americans in Saigon when I put this question to them. The Americans believe that the

South Vietnamese would feel that they had been betrayed and sold out to the enemy if such negotiations were to take place. Negotiations with the Vietcong could only imply that the USA were prepared to regard the 'National Liberation Front', i.e. the Vietcong, as a partner in negotiations and thus also as a future political force in South Vietnam. For the South Vietnamese government this would mean sitting down at the same table with their deadly enemy and admitting that this enemy might have a potential role in the future of South Vietnam.

I had the impression, however, that the Americans did not want to rule out the possibility of negotiations with the Vietcong, though as long as such negotiations are flatly rejected by the South Vietnamese government, the Americans would be running the risk of being deprived of their footing in South Vietnam as soon as they made a move to get into direct contact with the Vietcong. If the Americans were to make such a move, they fear that there would be a risk of the South Vietnamese renouncing American aid, expelling American troops and making a political about-turn to seek unity with the communists themselves. Any such link-up could result in a severe defeat.

The South Vietnam conditions for a peace treaty are as follows:

North Vietnam must cease its subversion and military activity in South Vietnam, withdraw their troops from the South and disband their front organisations in the South (i.e. the 'National Liberation Front' and the Vietcong);

The South Vietnamese must be allowed to administer their own affairs according to democratic principles and without any outside interference;

As soon as aggression from the North comes to an end, the Saigon government together with her allies will discontinue hostilities and request her allies to withdraw their troops;

The independence and freedom of the peoples of South Vietnam must be unconditionally guaranteed.

The South Vietnamese therefore still insist that the 'National Liberation Front' and the Vietcong must be liquidated.

Even these conditions, however, were formulated a long time ago—long before Mr Dong envisaged negotiations with the Vietcong in the presence of American troops in South Vietnam. It is perhaps not totally improbable that, after such a substantial compromise on the part of the Vietcong, the South Vietnamese government might also one day be prepared to compromise.

At all events there is continual and very intensive diplomatic activity in progress which suggests that the Americans may be exploring this line of approach. For the Americans there is ultimately only one condition for peace in Vietnam: South Vietnam must not be allowed to fall into the hands of the communists. And they naturally fear that if the 'National Liberation Front' were given too much of a voice in the negotiations it might result in a strong communist infiltration into South Vietnam and finally a communist seizure of power.

Is there any way of ensuring against this? This may well be the crucial question the Americans are asking themselves when they consider the suggestion to negotiate directly with the Vietcong. So far the USA seems to believe that there is only one real guarantee for ousting communism from South Vietnam: decisive military intervention.

But above all there now appear to be new, major and possibly insurmountable obstacles building up in South Vietnam. Mr Dong may have been putting out peace feelers in Helsinki for the very reason that the Vietcong themselves were anticipating, namely that strong units of the regular North Vietnamese army are now moving down to join battle in South Vietnam. The course of the war can therefore no longer be decided by the Vietcong alone. We may even suspect that North Vietnam sent in her troops because Hanoi wants to prevent the Vietcong from taking the initiative towards a peace settlement.

After the first hard blows dealt by the American troops against the Vietcong, I was told in Saigon: 'We [the Americans] reckon that the Vietcong will alter their tactics in the near future. They will give up attacking in large units. With these tactics they run the risk of rapid annihilation. That is why we think that the Vietcong will now start to organise hundreds of small-scale raids.'

The Americans were in fact rather apprehensive of such a change of tactics. A large army is at a disadvantage when operating against small raiding parties. But things have turned out otherwise. Reinforced by the prompt dispatch—whether asked for or not—of regular units from North Vietnam, the communists are now finally trying to engage the Americans in major frontal attacks. Their motive is obvious —in spite of their own enormous losses they are aiming at as high a rate of American casualties as possible, and the communists have frequently made clear what they expect from such a strategy: a revulsion of American public opinion against this war. Under the pressure of public opinion the U S government would then be forced to submit to negotiations under unfavourable conditions.

The Americans, on the other hand, want to avoid this very development. They too are decided to deal the enemy a decisive military blow that will force him to lower his price for peace. And this is why both sides are so stubbornly continuing their fight; both of them still hope that the opponent will be forced to give up the struggle for the same reason: the realisation that victory is impossible.

21

My departure from Saigon was very like my arrival. After so much time spent with the American and South Vietnamese troops and with USOM in the front line, Saigon seemed an island of peace, of pulsating life, a unique mixture of Asia and France.

My car was borne out to the airport on a stream of traffic. Only the relatively large numbers of jeeps and army trucks, amidst the hundreds of small taxis, motorised three-wheeled rickshaws and bicycles, were a reminder of the war—like the strict check on Vietnamese civilians entering the airport. The streets were lined with posters urging one not only to buy Lambrettas and Vespas, Phillips and Grundig, but to fly to France and the USA, to take a trip to the Italian cathedrals and the Edinburgh Festival. The airport buildings were packed with Vietnamese, some of them, perhaps, off to take up these pleasant invitations. All of them—provided they have completed their military service—can get passports and exit visas without any trouble.

The headlines of newspapers on the airport kiosks announce Vietcong successes and their leading articles criticise the government. The customs officers passed our baggage without examination, the man from the exchange control department collected our currency declaration slips without so much as a glance at them. The present Vietnamese government certainly has its dictatorial aspects, but in many ways South Vietnam is a free country. As our queue of passengers formed up at the passport desk, the official had not yet appeared. He arrived after half an hour's delay, soaking wet from a sudden tropical downpour. He calmly took off his shoes, wrung out his socks over the wastepaper basket, carefully hung them on a line, took a towel and comb from a drawer, dried his face and hair, looked into the mirror and combed his hair. Only then was he ready to attend to us.

As one of my American acquaintances had said the day before: 'The

Vietnamese are fighting for the French way of life.' Although this only applies to the towns, it was not until I was aboard the Air Vietnam plane waiting on the runway that I was once more reminded of the reality of war: we waited with motors running for permission to take off while no fewer than six squadrons of American jet bombers, their wings spiked with rockets, took off in front of us on a raid. Even after we took off, the pilot carefully steered the plane at a sharp angle to avoid the edge of the jungle where, as I knew, the Vietcong had launched an attack only the day before.